10 SUNDAY SCHOOLS THAT DARED TO CHANGE

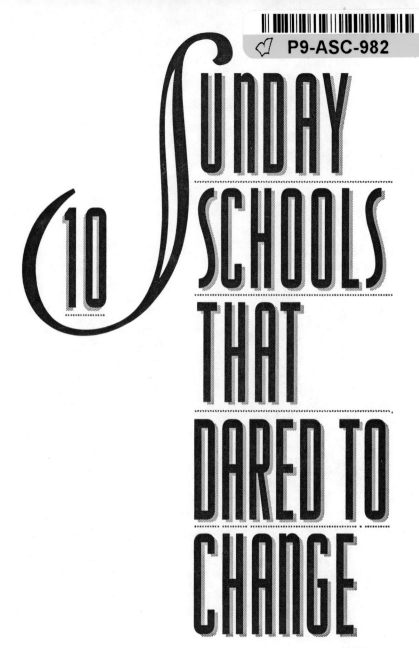

10 SUNDAY SCHOOLS THAT DARED TO CHANGE

HOW CHURCHES ACROSS AMERICA ARE CHANGING PARADIGMS TO REACH A NEW GENERATION

ELMER L. TOWNS

Regal Books
A Division of Gospel Light
Ventura, California, U.S.A.

Published by Regal Books
A Division of Gospel Light
Ventura, California, U.S.A.
Printed in U.S.A.

Regal Books is a ministry of Gospel Light, an evangelical Christian publisher dedicated to serving the local church. We believe God's vision for Gospel Light is to provide church leaders with biblical, user-friendly materials that will help them evangelize, disciple and minister to children, youth and families.

It is our prayer that this Regal Book will help you discover biblical truth for your own life and help you meet the needs of others. May God richly bless you.

For a free catalog of resources from Regal Books/Gospel Light please contact your Christian supplier or call 1-800-4-GOSPEL.

Library of Congress Cataloging-in-Publication Data
Towns, Elmer L.
     Ten Sunday schools that dared to change / Elmer L. Towns.
         p.   cm.
     ISBN 0-8307-1588-6
     1. Sunday schools—United States. 2. Sunday schools—Growth.
I. Title. II. Title: 10 Sunday schools that dared to change.
BV1516.A1T68 1993
268'.0973—dc20   93-14112
                                                            CIP

Rights for publishing this book in other languages are contracted by Gospel Literature International (GLINT). GLINT also provides technical help for the adaptation, translation and publishing of Bible study resources and books in scores of languages worldwide. For further information, contact GLINT, P.O. Box 4060, Ontario, CA 91761-1003, U.S.A., or the publisher.

Contents

Preface

Dr. Elmer L. Towns,
Liberty University

To me, the greatest Sunday School teacher in the world was the man who reached me for Jesus Christ and became an influential teacher in my life.

Jimmy Breland was an unassuming man with simple likes and purposes in life. In 1938, he was a Jewel Tea & Coffee salesman in Savannah, Georgia, trying to make a living near the end of the Great Depression. I was five years old when I met him in the living room of our home where we had moved recently. Breland was showing my mother various kinds of coffee and tea. When he saw me, he said, "Would you like to go to Sunday School?"

"What's Sunday School?" I asked in my childlike simplicity. I had been taught to respect adults and to be polite. So, my question was not intended to be sarcastic or belligerent. It was simply a request for information.

"Sunday School is where you have fun," Breland answered with a twinkle in his eye. This skinny six-foot-tall man had an Adam's apple that stuck out over his tie. It bounced when he talked.

"Sunday School is a place where we sing, tell stories and have a lot of fun." His enthusiasm was infectious. "We even have a sand table. We'll make a sand mountain, and I'll show you how Jesus walked across the mountains." Breland used his two fingers to simulate a man walking.

Wow, a sand table, I thought. In my childish bewilderment I asked, "Doesn't the sand fall off?"

"We have a ledge to keep it on," Breland answered. He proceeded to tell me that a mirror could be used to create a lake. Again, with his walking fingers, he showed how Jesus would walk across the top of the water.

"He walked on water?" I remember exclaiming. Then, turning

to my mother, I blurted, "I want to go to Sunday School. I want to go to Sunday School."

Being a thoughtful and protective mother, she asked the coffee salesman, "What kind of Sunday School are you talking about?"

Breland's answer was a deliberate one. "The Eastern Heights Presbyterian Church is an outstanding place to learn the Word of God."

My mother probably was concerned that he was recruiting me for a cult. However, she had been married in a small Presbyterian church in South Carolina and was willing to grant permission for me to attend. She then asked where the church was located.

When Breland told her it was about five miles away, across town, mother hesitated. "He's such a little boy. He would get lost walking five miles to Sunday School."

Breland turned and pointed through the screen door to a large, black panel truck. The words "Jewel Tea & Coffee" were inscribed on the side. "You wanna ride in my truck to Sunday School?" he asked me.

"I wanna ride in the truck," I begged my mother. "I wanna ride in the big, black truck."

Mother, however, pointed out that I would be in a strange crowd. She also was concerned that I might wander into the open fields that surrounded the church. So, she compromised. "He can go to Sunday School when he goes to the first grade."

"I'll come back and get you then," Breland promised. Each time he came to sell coffee, he reminded me, "Don't forget you are going to Sunday School with me when you go to the first grade."

Three or four months later in September 1938, I entered the first grade and was primed to take my first trip to Sunday School. On a rainy Sunday morning, I was dressed in white short pants and stood on the top step waiting for Breland. He soon arrived, his black panel truck splashing through the mud.

I ran through the light rain to the back of the truck, wondering where I would sit among the coffee boxes. But much to my surprise, the truck was empty when Breland opened the back door. I sat on the floor as he drove to the next street to pick up the four Amar boys. He then drove five blocks and picked up the two Drigger children. Then he cut through a housing project and gathered other children en route to Sunday School.

Breland picked me up every week for 14 years, and I did not miss a Sunday. My mother encouraged me to obtain a perfect-attendance pin along with other children and warned me not to skip school and play if I intended to go to Sunday School.

One morning I told my mother that I was sick and could not attend. "You're not sick," she responded. "You just feel that way. If you stay at home, you will have to take castor oil."

So, I went to Sunday School and was awarded a gold pin for one year of perfect attendance, a gold wreath for the second and a bar for every year thereafter.

When I was in the third grade, I was standing in front of the church one Sunday morning when Breland pointed to a man tapping a cigarette before lighting up for a smoke.

"Don't ever smoke," he said.

"Why not?"

"It's dumb. Smoking wastes money."

That advice came from a man who hated to spend money. He never owned a house, but lived in a garage apartment or a housing project. He bragged that he never bought a car in his life, always driving a company truck because it saved money. The company paid for the truck, insurance and put gas in the tank as well.

"You might as well get you some grass (which was not mar-

ijuana in those days) and roll your own in a dollar bill and burn
it up," Breland said. "You like to burn up dollar bills?"

"Not me," I responded, despite the fact that my mother had
smoked when she was young, my father smoked and all of my
uncles on both sides of the family were smokers. But I never
smoked, because of Breland.

Two weeks later, Breland continued the conversation. He
pointed to two men who wanted to be church officers but
couldn't because they drank alcoholic beverages. Then Breland
turned to the group of boys where I was standing and said,
"Don't ever take your first drink of liquor."

"Why not?" I asked, being the inquisitive member of the
crowd.

Breland did not preach morality. Rather, his answer reflected
his frugal life-style. "Drinking wastes a lot of money," he said. Then
with a twinkle in his eye, he reasoned, "You may as well take that
bottle to the commode and pour your money away." Turning to
me, he asked, "You like to pour money down the toilet?"

"Not me," I said.

All of my uncles on mother's side of the family were hard-
liquor-drinking Southern dirt farmers. My father was an
alcoholic and died of cirrhosis of the liver and cancer,
but I never took a drink, because of Breland.

The power of Sunday School is still in the teacher who influ-
ences students. This book points out that when teachers become
interested in academic content and delivering lessons by lecturing, the entire Sunday School lessens its influence on the church
and society. But most of all, the Sunday School fails to influence the lives of those who attend.

I was one of the approximately 25 students in Breland's Sunday School class. About 19 of us entered full-time Christian service. We became associated with a variety of denominations,

including Southern Baptist, Freewill Baptist, Presbyterian, Christian Ministerial Alliance and Pentecostal Holiness.

Three were college presidents. Others became foreign missionaries or taught in Christian day schools. Dr. Frank Perry pastored one of the largest Southern Baptist churches while in north Atlanta, and Dr. Albert Freundt became professor of church history at the Reformed Presbyterian Seminary.

We were children from poor homes, yet we never thought of ourselves as being economically deprived. We had a Sunday School teacher who lit a fire and gave us a vision of what we could do. Breland made us believe that although we were average people with limited resources and faced difficult obstacles, we could climb mountains with God's help.

The message of the 10 Sunday Schools discussed in this book is that the teacher must cast a vision in the hearts of pupils. When that happens, the flame will be rekindled for the glory of God.

These Sunday Schools are not doing anything new. They are basically taking yesterday's vision that was grounded in eternity and are accomplishing the task by using modern tools.

I want to thank staff members of Gospel Light for their encouragement in preparing this book. Also, thanks to Linda Murphrey, Vanessa Van Eaton and Linda Barkley for typing the manuscript.

And thanks to Jimmy Breland, who introduced me to Sunday School and helped mould my character and outlook on life.

Sincerely yours in Christ,
Elmer L. Towns
Summer 1993
Lynchburg, Virginia

Introduction

SUNDAY SCHOOLS ARE LIKE SAILING SHIPS. IF THE SAILS ARE trimmed properly and the navigation is correct, the ship has a better opportunity to reach its destination.

Unfortunately, most Sunday Schools in America are adrift, foundering or headed in the wrong direction. Some are becalmed. Others are equipped to move but have not trimmed their sails to catch the winds of opportunity or have veered off course.

We must turn those misguided vessels around if we expect to reach the objective. If they are redirected and catch a vision, their sails will fill and they will grow internally and externally. They will join a small but adventuresome fleet of Sunday Schools, ships that are on course, moving, growing, and charting a future that is bright indeed.

This section introduces 10 models, drawing examples from existing churches, that will change and revitalize the Sunday Schools of America.

Models of the Future

The First Baptist Church in Arlington, Texas, found itself land-locked in the aging downtown heart of the city. Approximately 1,500 people were crowding into facilities that could not be expanded. To make matters worse, the Sunday-morning drive to church was much like running an obstacle course. But a few leaders turned those problems into chariot wheels that rode over barriers.

Because people wouldn't come to the Sunday School, Tillie Burgin challenged the church to take the Sunday School to the people.

Today, more than 134 mission Sunday Schools/Bible studies meet in various locations (mostly apartment buildings) throughout greater Arlington.

Dedicated lay members, in the spirit of Sunday School founder Robert Raikes, take Sunday School to pupils. Workers walk through an apartment complex gathering people for Sunday School that meets in any available space, including areas around a swimming pool and in a recreational room. At approximately 11:00 A.M. people begin singing Christian songs, teaching the Word of God and fulfilling the original purpose for Sunday School in their apartment complex.

Many plateaued Sunday Schools can grow again by taking Sunday School to the people.

The children's classes of Highlands Community Church instituted learning centers that focus on activity, excitement and Bible learning. Rather than telling stories and giving children pictures to color, members of this Sunday School in greater Seattle, Washington, made learning fun.

Learning is deeper and longer lasting when it is fun, action-oriented and Bible-based.

Pastor Rick Warren tried to build the largest Sunday School in California at the Saddleback Valley Community Church, which is about 40 miles south of downtown Los Angeles. He discovered, however, that the typical California suburbanite in the 1990s was not enamored with the traditional Sunday School. Although he built a large worship service, Sunday School was not "clicking" with the Southern California lifestyle.

Warren changed the orientation from the traditional Sunday School curriculum. Now, the adult curriculum emphasizes communicating skills and Christian maturity that every new believer must acquire to live and serve Jesus Christ. The curriculum is growth-graded to take people from their unsaved state to salvation, to growth in knowledge and finally to where they can reach out to others.

Warren said that another curriculum book is always waiting to be covered in the traditional Sunday School. In the Saddleback church's new Sunday School curriculum strategy, a student does not move on until he learns skills and attitudes. A person graduates when he reaches the final course of study. He is equipped to be a teacher, to lead others through the process.

This "Sunday School process" does not take place on Sunday morning but in the evening, afternoon and morning from Monday through Saturday in rented schools, convention centers and in other church and school facilities as well.

Sunday Schools must be purpose-driven to teach life-changing skills and Christian maturity.

Pastor Bill Monroe planted the Florence Baptist Temple in Florence, South Carolina, in 1969. He built a congregation of more than 1,400, using buses to reach children and a large auditorium Bible class to reach adults.

He faced a barrier, however, when the Bible class attendance reached 400 and the church attendance grew to 1,400. After some strategy changes, the church is growing again.

The adult Bible class has been broken into groups of approximately 10 each. The new classes produce more adult leadership because many adults are leading Bible studies.

When the church was primarily a busing church, workers went to the front door of a home to invite people to ride a bus to Sunday School. Now, most people drive to church because Sunday School enrollment is emphasized and workers approach prospects by asking, "May we enroll you in Bible study?"

Monroe views outreach as a conveyor belt of influence that moves people from being a prospect to enrolling in Sunday School, to becoming believers, to becoming disciples and then to being trained to reach others.

An emphasis on Sunday School enrollment will create a new loyalty of pupils to their classes.

"We do everything through the Sunday School," said Pastor Edwin Young of The Second Baptist Church in Houston, Texas. That church, however, does not follow the traditional age-graded and gender-graded classes of approximately 10 adults found in Southern Baptist churches. The church has adult classes of 30 to more than 200 people that are organized to involve everyone in ministry and growth. Each class has a man and woman teacher, who teach on alternate weeks, plus an assortment of leaders and workers.

Just as the body grows by the division of cells, so the church grows by adding new adult Sunday School cells that bond members to one another and to the class purpose.

Churches thrive when adult classes delegate total ministry to their members.

Because the First Assembly of God in Phoenix, Arizona, was

unable to expand, it left the south-side neighborhoods where it had been successful in the Sunday School bus ministry and built a sanctuary in the northern section of the city.

But the church did not abandon the south side. Pastor Tommy Barnett motivated his workers to create multiple Sunday School bus routes to serve those south-side neighborhoods on Saturday morning, Saturday afternoon and Sunday morning by using such available space as rented public schools and picnic tables in city parks. The church also purchased houses where children were taught the Word of God.

Because Sunday School workers could not create a permanent bond between the child and the church, the students and their parents now are bused to the facilities on the north side for special events. Every week the children's parents are bused to the church for a Sunday night service. This megachurch of more than 10,000 has shown an innovative approach to solve time and space logistical problems.

Taking Sunday School to the streets will reinforce its original evangelistic purpose.

The Grove City Nazarene Church is located on the south edge of Columbus, Ohio. At one time its Sunday School of 250 people was so crowded it could not grow. Pastor Bob Huffaker suggested adding a Sunday evening school.

Now, beginning at 6:00 P.M., families attend a unified worship service and then break into age-categorized classes to study God's Word. The evening Sunday School attendance has shown steady growth over the morning Sunday School, but new space has provided explosive growth for the Sunday morning worship crowd. Also, the evening Sunday School is much larger than the previous evening preaching service.

Visitors traditionally attend a worship service rather than a

Sunday School. Leaders know that the best fishing for prospects is in the "worship pool," having a view of attracting them to Sunday School. Today, the Grove City Nazarene Church concentrates on outreach Sunday mornings and on discipleship Sunday evenings.

ℬy meeting Sunday evening, the Sunday School can provide a better foundation for the total church ministry.

The Skyline Wesleyan Church in Lemon Grove, California, was committed to growth but was short of facilities to meet the increased attendance that resulted from evangelistic outreach. So additional time for three more Sunday Schools was added on Sunday mornings and a fifth Sunday School is being considered for Saturday night. Attendance has grown from 1,000 to 4,000 during the past decade.

ℐn an age of spiraling building costs, multiple meeting times on Sunday morning provides space for continued evangelism and growth.

Pastor Knute Larson does not follow the traditional American church organizational pattern of small-group Bible study and larger attended worship services at The Chapel in Akron, Ohio. The people meet in *cells* for small-group intimacy during the week and large crowds gather for *celebration* at the worship service. The *congregational* function is served by Adult Bible Fellowships, which is their term for adult Sunday School, but the focus is fellowship and Bible study. The adult classes have been reconstituted from lecture-driven centers to opportunities for Bible study and fellowship.

Whereas morning worship attracts people to a church, people bond to the church through relationships and Bible study.

Pastor Larry Lamb saw the explosive multiplication of condominiums and houses for baby boomers north of San Diego, California, and knew the traditional American church would not reach them. He envisioned a nontraditional church that was seeker sensitive and user friendly, yet evangelical in doctrine and evangelistic in thrust. He planned a "Vision Day" to communicate the unique methods of such a church so that everyone would be on the same starting line in the new venture.

Sunday Schools can be revitalized by a new vision of expectations and perception.

My uncle Gene was a small-time farmer who understood what it took to break out of the rut, although he personally never did. As a barefoot boy picking cotton for a penny a pound, I remember him telling me: "If you always do what you've always done, you'll always be where you've always been."

From Rut to Roots

Sunday Schools will not turn around if we continue in the rut into which we have fallen, even if the Sunday School becomes more effective and uses better-trained teachers. Let's not try to improve our rut. Let's do Sunday School differently. Let's return to the original roots of Sunday School. Let's turn it around!

If Sunday School is a sailing ship that is dead in the water, getting a better helmsman, a better rigger and better sails will not make the vessel sail any better. We need to find the breeze to get us moving. We need some changes.

The Sunday Schools of America can sail again, but we need something more than improved teaching methods, extensive teacher preparation or better facilities.

Many people perceive Sunday School as a place where teachers talk and pupils listen. The problem is perception. Many people perceive teachers as teachers, pupils as pupils and the Sunday School as a school.

This book suggests that we no longer call them teachers but leaders. We should no longer call it teaching but Bible study. We don't need to improve expectations and perceptions. We need to change expectations and perception.

New Models, New Perceptions

Twenty-five years ago I wrote *The Ten Largest Sunday Schools and What Made Them Grow*, which became a best-seller. According to *Christian Life* editor, Robert Walker, the book "hit the American church like a thunder clap." That book described 10 churches as models for the revitalization of all Sunday Schools in America. The book created new perceptions of Sunday School.

The message was that Sunday Schools could be revitalized by aggressive evangelistic outreach, by door-to-door visitation, by busing and by improving traditional teaching methods. That book helped revitalize many churches and introduced America to the megachurch; but it suggested only one model.

This book is different. It suggests many models for revitalizing the Sunday Schools of the '90s. No one prescription will work in every situation. As you read this volume, watch for the model that best matches your community and church. Only one gospel saves and doctrine never changes, but methods vary from culture to culture. For example, Sunday School busing has not worked in the Andes Mountains or in the Amazon jungle.

Methods also vary from age to age. Sunday School busing

did not work 300 years ago when modern highways were not in existence nor vehicles to move the masses over great distances.

Models of Innovation

Each of the first 10 chapters presents a model of innovation for Sunday School revitalization and growth. The Sunday School in each chapter is described to support a group of principles.

Each chapter offers a ministry application section to explain the strategy and principle of the Sunday School described in that chapter. The chapter is *descriptive* (what has been done) the application is *prescriptive* (how to do it).

May God use the description of the energies of many Sunday School workers mentioned in this book to revitalize other workers. Let us pray for a Sunday School revival in America.

1
Sunday School with a Mission

First Baptist Church
Arlington, Texas

Dr. Charles Wade, Pastor

Tillie Burgin,
Minister of Missions

$\mathcal{A}$ DECADE AGO, THE FIRST BAPTIST CHURCH IN DOWNTOWN Arlington, Texas, arrived at a crossroads.

The church was located next door to the massive University of Texas-Arlington. Many families who once lived in the area had moved to the suburbs and were hesitant to return for Sunday services because of obstacles to such a commute.

Church growth slowed and by the early 1980s Sunday School attendance had leveled off at 1,500.

Going to the Mountain

In response, Dr. Charles Wade, the pastor, and Tillie Burgin, missions director, developed a plan to take weekly Bible studies to apartment complexes. An old adage says, "If you can't bring 'em to the mountain, you take the mountain to them."

A decade later, Sunday School attendance rose to nearly 4,000. The traditional way to accomplish that growth might have been a bus ministry. Wade, however, pointed out that the downtown facilities could not have accommodated that growth.

Families Also Reached

Bus ministry in most churches reaches children, but the Arlington ministry reaches children and their families. The mixture of children, youth and adults reflects the ratio in most Sunday Schools. Children are the focus, but adults are the foundation.

Years earlier, Arlington church members had visited outlying areas and invited children to Sunday School to hear the Word of God. Now, more than 300 workers travel to 134 apartment complexes to lead weekly Bible studies, taking the Bible to "where people are" in what is now referred to as the Arlington Mission.

"We Don't Call It Sunday School"

"We don't call it Sunday School," Tillie said. "The folks where we minister don't understand what Sunday School is. So, we call it Bible study."

When pressed for a definition, she says that a Bible study is like a church, but not a church. "We do it 7 days a week, 24 hours a day. It's not a Sunday happening, although the people come together to study the Word of God on Sunday."

The First Baptist Church belongs to the Southern Baptist Convention, an association of almost 40,000 churches and 3,800 missions, which will become churches. Technically, the 134 Bible studies in Arlington do not count on the Southern Baptist list because they are not constituted missions.

"We do everything for the people that a church does," said Tillie, who conducts visitors on Sunday morning "Tillie Tours." During that time, she describes each Bible study to visitors as "their church."

Using Available Facilities

Plans are not being made to construct buildings for the Bible studies, she said. "We use what we have. We study the Bible around swimming pools, in recreation rooms, laundry rooms or even in empty apartments.

"Some of them meet in mobile home parks. Many apartment managers see the great life-changing influence on people and loan us empty apartments that are not rented out. Sometimes, apartment managers are the biggest supporters we have."

One Baptist associational worker suggested to Tillie, "You're not a church!"

"As far as the Lord is concerned, we are," Tillie answered. "We've got believers who are assembled together. That's a body of believers that we call a church."

Because the Sunday Schools may meet by the pool, in the laundry room of an apartment complex, around a picnic table in a mobile home, or in rented storefront buildings, she refers to those locations as "the property."

Some of the Bible studies move around weekly. Like children playing hopscotch, they move from one sidewalk to another. So in the same way, the mission Sunday Schools are not described by a building but as a group of people.

One Mission Now a Church

One of the groups became a church when it organized itself from missions status into a local Baptist church. But that is not the plan for the Bible studies. Tillie pointed out that approximately 90 to 95 percent of the people in the Bible studies do not attend church anywhere. "This is their church," she said. "The workers are Bible study leaders or you can call them pastors."

"I used to think that men were pastors and that ladies were Bible study leaders," said Tillie, who then told a story based on her years as a Southern Baptist foreign missionary. "One day in the middle of a Bible study, a little baby died. Immediately, they got me and I came quickly. When I got there the people asked, 'Can Virginia, the Bible study leader, bury our baby?' Virginia looked at me and said, 'Can I?' Before I could answer, the people said, 'Virginia's the only pastor we've ever had.'"

Leaders Are Considered Pastors

Regardless of what leaders are called, Tillie said, the most important thing is what they do. Whether they are called chaplains, Bible study leaders or pastors, they are a group of lay people doing ministry 7 days a week, 24 hours a day in leading people to study God's Word, to know Jesus Christ and to meet their spiritual needs. "They are pastors and this is church," she concluded.

Many leaders of the Bible studies are seminary students, lawyers and workers at the First Baptist Church in Arlington. Because of the success of this multifaceted outreach, workers have come from other churches in the area simply because they believe in the task.

Missions in Action

The activities of each Bible study are similar. First, the workers arrive around 10:00 A.M. and begin going door-to-door to invite people to the Bible study. Formerly, bus workers would visit on Saturday morning and invite people to ride the bus on Sunday morning. The appeal now is for immediate response that morning.

At many of the Bible studies in empty apartments, people sit on the floor. Some sit in chairs around a pool or in the chairs of a recreation room.

Everyone Attends Worship

"Worship is first," Tillie explained. Everyone attends worship, including the children. They sing, using tape recorders, portable keyboards, guitars or whatever musical instruments are available to the people at the time. The offering is usually taken during this time, including announcements, followed by special music. Each group reports the amount of an offering to the First Baptist Church but retains the offering to use in local ministry.

After approximately 15 to 20 minutes, the group breaks into age divisions for Bible study. Usually, this means a children's group, a youth group and an adult Bible study.

"I tell them to begin with John 3:16 for the adults," Tillie said. "If they stay close to John 3:16, it will bring people to Jesus Christ and develop the group." Tillie says a group can spend a year studying and applying John 3:16, but it may move to other areas. The workers themselves write the children's material.

Attire No Longer an Excuse

The church has eliminated the excuse that many people give: "I don't have anything to wear." The workers have done a good job of convincing people they don't have to dress up for Bible study.

A training session is scheduled for all workers at 4:00 P.M. Sunday. "That's the most important time of the week," Tillie said. "We don't take anything away from focus on the Scriptures that is to be taught by the workers. It's worship time for us."

The training session begins with music, both special music and group singing. Workers then share testimonies of what occurred during studies that day. They pray.

"Then they fill out the numbers," Tillie said. This involves the amount of offering, attendance of children, youth and adults and other pertinent information.

Ministry Potential Unlimited

When asked how large the ministry is expected to grow, Tillie said, "It's according to how many workers we have. If we can get workers, it is easy to find the property and to get a Bible study started.

"We have approximately 350 to 400 volunteers right now. I don't ask people to come down and help. Most people don't respond to that type of appeal. They come to see what's going on and I give them a specific job. I ask them to help with the teaching, leading, singing or knocking on doors to get people to attend. Most of our volunteers come as a result of prayer."

One person who had worked at a local manufacturing plant testified that he had attended a traditional Sunday School class.

He said it appeared as though things were being repeated Sunday after Sunday, that he was listening to a talk, then going home. One day he asked his Sunday School teacher, "Why don't we do stuff like Jesus did?" A hush came over the class.

"Do you know Tillie Burgin?" the teacher asked.

"No."

Visitor Takes "Tillie Tour"

"Tillie has a mission in this church, but I don't know what it is called. I want you to go with her on Sunday to take the 'Tillie Tour.'"

That day after touring three or four apartments, the visitor said later, "I have never seen anything like this, people sitting on the floor, singing, clapping and listening to the Word of God. It really inspired me to do something, so I got involved." Today, he is a Bible study leader with his own Sunday School, his own "property."

When asked if he wanted to be a pastor, he said, "I don't want to go through seminary or anything like that. I just want to take care of the people in my apartment building, bury the dead, lead people to Christ, baptize them when they get saved and teach them the Word of God every week."

A worker named Tom was asked about his ministry each Sunday. "Is it Bible study or is it preaching that you do?"

"We compress the Word of God together and we do Sunday School and church together. I don't know what you call it, I just do it."

Testimony of Changed Lives

Many of the apartment managers support Tillie because they see the change in the lives of those who attend the Bible studies. They have seen Tillie carrying groceries to the poor and on occasions she has paid their rent. Many apartment managers will loan her the key to an empty apartment for a Bible study for as long as the apartment is unrented.

"We have been moved five times in five weeks," Tillie said. On some occasions, the Bible study has had to pay rent because all of the apartments were occupied in the apartment complex.

Leader of the Band

Tillie Burgin was called "Leader of the Band" in the May-June 1991 issue of *Mission U.S.A.*, a magazine published by the Southern Baptist Home Mission Board. "Born a block from the center—called Mission Arlington—Burgin now conducts a fine-tuned orchestra of volunteers playing to an audience of physically and spiritually hungry Texans," the magazine reported.

The Sunday morning outreach began when Burgin became the church's missions director. Because great works always grow out of great vision, the vision she had for the unchurched, unsaved neighborhood in which she grew up became the driving force that produced the outreach of more than 2,000 people each week.

Study Began in Apartment

The magazine tells how the first Bible study was begun in Virginia Maanani's apartment. Virginia and two teenage daughters moved to Arlington from New York to escape what she said was an abusive husband. Virginia, who was having financial problems, said she was afraid to let Tillie enter her apartment the first time she called. "I thought she was a bill collector or someone coming to evict me."

Later that day, Tillie returned with four bags of groceries

and came back the next week with a check for the rent. Then she paid the electric bill. Virginia recalled that Tillie "would just pop in sometimes to say how she cared about us."

Mission Becomes Her Life

With the help of Mission Arlington and Tillie Burgin, Virginia Maanani turned around spiritually and financially. She was able to move into a duplex, but she still returns to the apartment complex to help in ministry. Virginia now leads two Bible studies. "This is not just a mission field," Virginia told *Mission U.S.A.* "It is my life."

In addition to the Sunday ministry, the mission helps 50 to 60 people who come daily seeking food, clothing, transportation to work or money for rent and utilities. The mission has a shelter for the homeless. It also has a "jobs office" where people call in search for day laborers. But beyond all that, counselors help people trapped in drugs, alcohol and other problems. A Bible study is conducted every morning. Of the 350 to 400 volunteers involved in Mission Arlington, approximately 200 lead Bible studies each Sunday.

Many people who live in the apartment complexes are single-parent women without fathers in the home. Therefore, many of the Bible studies plan an afternoon "Fun Day" where the leaders play with the children and help them with their homework. Sometimes a "Fun Day" is scheduled on Saturday and workers visit every apartment. At other times the event takes place on Wednesday afternoon.

Two Hundred Bible Studies Formed

When people are saved, they usually become more responsible. As a result, many apartment managers see a change in the way those people care for the facilities.

Tillie said there are approximately 3,000 apartment complexes in the greater Arlington area with only 200 Bible studies, which she considers is too few. Two years ago she said she knew of 14 apartment complexes awaiting a Bible study. All she needed to start them were volunteers.

Sunday School has been defined as "The reaching, teaching, winning and nurturing arm of the church."

Conclusion

Sunday School has been defined as "the reaching, teaching, winning and nurturing arm of the church." The outreach of First Baptist Church in Arlington, Texas, certainly fits that description. However, the reaching arm is so unusual that it could trigger a revival in America if every church would follow its example.

When people won't come to Sunday School, perhaps Sunday School should be taken to the people. When that is done, it will revitalize the American church and will make an impact on our cities for Christ.

Ministry Application

Tillie Burgin had difficulty expressing whether Mission Arlington was a church mission, a mission Sunday School, a chapel, a church plant or simply an outreach ministry.

Dr. Larry Lewis, president of the Southern Baptist Home Mission Board, considers them outreach units. The following definitions will help the reader identify different kinds of outreach ministry.

Outreach Defined

1. Synonyms: In addition to being called a mission Sunday School, the Sunday morning outreach could be referred to as a branch Sunday School, an outreach Sunday School, a chapel Sunday School or a new church that is beginning as a Sunday School.

2. Definitions: A mission Sunday School may fall within the following organizational structures for church outreach.

a. A geographically extended parish—Technically, this is one church that is located in more than one place and ministers to more than one group of people. It has more than one central core of pastoral ministries, yet possesses a unity of direction, governance, leadership and control. It is a church situated on several sites that can be used for Sunday School. (NOTE: For further study, see *Ten Innovative Churches,* 1991, Regal Books, by Elmer Towns. Chapter 16 discusses the concept.)

b. A multicongregational church—A mission Sunday School also fits within the framework of a multicongregational church, which is defined as multiple centers of ministries, multiple staff and multiple places of ministry.

c. Expansion church growth—Starting a new work in another location among the same type of people for the same purpose.

d. Extended church growth—Beginning a similar type of church among a different type of people (i.e., cross-cultural evangelism) or a different kind of church and the same kind of people.

Historical Notes

In 1780, Robert Raikes began the modern-day Sunday School movement in Glouchester, England. He gathered approximately 90 boys into Mrs. Meredith's kitchen and paid her a shilling to teach them "readin', ritin', numbers and religion."

During the next 50 years, 1.5 million people were enrolled in Sunday School in England. By that time, the Sunday School movement had leaped the Atlantic into the newly established United States and began spreading rapidly.

In England and America, the establishment of new Sunday Schools is similar to those started by Tillie Burgin, except the early Sunday Schools were not connected to a local church.

It is difficult to determine just when Sunday Schools were connected with local church outreach. In 1829, Francis Scott Key in his inaugural address as president of the American Sunday School Union challenged the organization to evangelize the "heathen" (his misapplied term) from Pittsburgh to the Rockies by what he termed the "Mississippi Valley Enterprise."

This was a campaign to send missionaries to establish mission Sunday Schools in every hamlet, paying the missionaries one dollar a day and supplying them with a horse and an endorsement. The missionaries would go to an unevangelized village and enroll children for Sunday School, then raise $10 for a hundred books that he would call a Sunday School library. The Mississippi Valley Enterprise, which started in 1829, led to the establishment of 61,299 Sunday Schools within the next 50 years.

The Scofield Memorial Church in Dallas, Texas, was pastored by the famous Rev. C. I. Scofield, editor of *The Scofield Reference Bible*. Beginning in the 1930s, this church attempted to plant 20 mission Sunday Schools around the city of Dallas with a view that each one would become like the mother church with a Bible-teaching outreach.

A few missions developed into full church status, such as Reinhart Bible Church and Faith Bible Church of West Dallas. (The author organized the Dennison Street Chapel, one of these mission Sunday Schools, into Faith Bible Church in 1956.)

One of the most aggressive Sunday School outreach ministries might have been the Highland Park Baptist Church, Chattanooga, Tennessee. That church was listed second among the 100 largest churches in America in the mid-'70s. Pastored by Dr. Lee Roberson, Highland Park reported an average weekly attendance of approximately 4,800 in 1968 at the main campus and at the 42 chapels.

The local Chattanooga paper ran a Sunday insert with a photograph of 13 churches that had previously been Sunday School missions of Highland Park Baptist Church. The paper reported that all 13 had become indigenous local churches affiliated with the Southern Baptist Convention.

Purpose, Objectives

The reason for starting mission Sunday Schools differs from church to church. The First Baptist Church in Arlington, Texas, did not intend to organize these ministries into local churches (even though one has become a local church). The intent was to establish Bible studies and centers for evangelistic outreach. Mission Sunday Schools seem to be extensions of the ministry of First Baptist Church into an apartment complex and/or mobile home park.

The following purposes for a missions Sunday School are suggested:

1. To reach children. Many churches see the need of reaching children in a poor economic class or in a different class from its own neighborhood. This may be a bus ministry, Bible study,

pastoral care or humanitarian outreach. When the author organized Faith Bible Church in a poor section of Dallas, Texas,
three or four other missions existed in the neighborhood. One

The four purposes for a missions Sunday School are to: reach children, evangelize an area, prepare for a church move and plant a church.

mission was famous for giving all the children of the neighborhood shoes every Christmas, along with a turkey dinner for
every family and coats for the cold weather of Dallas. Children
from my mission always went to that mission to obtain these
items.

2. To evangelize an area. Certain mission Sunday Schools
are begun with the view of evangelistic outreach into a new area.
In addition to teaching the Bible, this new center of outreach
follows either the pattern of extended church growth or expanded church growth.

3. To prepare for a church move. Some churches have
planned to move into a new neighborhood and have begun a
mission Sunday School with a view of ultimately moving the
entire church into the neighborhood. The Wallace Memorial
Presbyterian Church at one time was located within the city
limits of Washington, D.C. During the late '50s, the church
made plans to move to a suburb in Maryland. Originally, a mission Sunday School was started on property purchased for that
purpose. Eventually, the entire church moved to the area.

4. To plant a church. Sometimes a church will begin a mission Sunday School with a view of a new church facility. The

Emmanuel Baptist Church located near downtown Fort Wayne, Indiana, followed this strategy in the '60s and '70s, planting nearly 20 churches in surrounding neighborhoods. The author was present at Emmanuel Baptist Church in 1968 when a group of people was formed as Blackhawk Baptist Church. They moved to an outlying neighborhood to begin a new church. At the time, the mother church was averaging less than 400 in attendance. Within a decade, Blackhawk Baptist Church was averaging more than 1,400.

Are Cells Biblical?

The book of Acts seemingly provides a biblical base for a model of one church that has many smaller units such as mission Sunday Schools.

Technically, this is called an extended geographical parish church or the multicongregational church. The church at Jerusalem was such a church.

"Now the multitude of those who believed were of one heart and one soul; neither did anyone say that any of the things he possessed was his own, but they had all things in common" (Acts 4:32). Note that the word "multitude" is singular in the original language; the church was one entity.

Later we are told that "believers were the more added to the Lord, multitudes both of men and women" (Acts 5:14, *KJV*). Here "multitudes" is plural in the original language, describing more than one entity. Those entities probably were small groups, classes or gatherings of people within the Jerusalem church. They could have been house churches (i.e., a church meeting in a house that is part of the larger city church.)

The Jerusalem church was one large group (celebration), and many smaller groups (cells). The leaders went from house to house (see Acts 2:46; 5:42). This was probably not door-to-door soul-winning, nor was it "every member canvassing." Each cell of the Jerusalem church met in different houses for fellowship and ministry.

Apparently the early Jerusalem church did not serve communion in a large gathering or celebration but served the Lord's table in small groups or cells that met in houses (see Acts 2:46). Thus, the large group in the Jerusalem church met for celebration, preaching, motivation and testimony (see Acts 3:11) and in small cells for fellowship, accountability, instruction and identity (see Acts 5:42).

From these observations, I conclude that the norm for the New Testament church included small cell groups and larger celebration groups.

The traditional American church met in large groups (celebration) for the Sunday morning worship service. The function of small groups was carried out primarily in small Sunday School classes. Today, however, new emerging churches are meeting in small groups in weeknight flocks, Bible classes or care groups.

Different churches have different emphases in their small groups. Some, such as New Hope Community Church in Portland, Oregon, emphasize fellowship and pastoral care through cell groups. Willow Creek Community Church of greater Chicago, Illinois, emphasizes Bible study; and Horizon Christian Fellowship of greater San Diego, California, emphasizes worship.

The church at Corinth also appeared to have several groups, as did the Jerusalem church, but the groups were wrongly divided. It appears that one group emphasized Paul, another Apollos and the self-proclaimed spiritual groups said they were of Christ (see 1 Cor. 1:12). Another group probably emphasized Peter (see 1 Cor. 3:22).

Several smaller groups or house churches in Corinth contributed to the division. Instead of leadership bringing the

Corinthian churches together, the churches apparently also were divided by geographical and/or ethnic lines.

When Paul wrote to the church at Rome from Corinth, he revealed the makeup of the Corinthian church. He greeted Priscilla and Aquilla and the church in their house (see Rom. 16:3-6). He mentioned "the churches of the Gentiles" (v.4), which may have consisted of house churches or cells having predominately Gentile members, meeting in the home of a Gentile (the homogeneous unit principle).

Paul also sent greetings from "the churches of Christ" (Rom. 16:16). The term "churches of Christ" is a descriptive phrase used to identify Jewish believers. The Greek term translated "Christ" was parallel to the Hebrew term "Messiah" or "Anointed One," the hope of the Jews.

Hence, the phrase "churches of Christ" may have been used to describe Jewish house churches (the homogeneous unity principle) in Corinth.

Paul concluded the chapter with "the whole church, saluteth you," (Rom. 16:23, *KJV*), a description of the total Corinthian church (the extended geographical parish church) of Jewish and Gentile home churches. One church meeting in many locations probably was a biblical expression of church organization.

After the New Testament was closed, those early manifestations of the extended geographical church usually ended up with a bishop over several churches. The mother church usually became a cathedral (probably not a biblical expression of church organization). In other ages, the attempt ended in denominational churches, each separate, but all united under one superstructure. In other words, many groups have tried to build large churches in many different geographical locations but with various results.

It remains to be seen whether present attempts to accomplish such a goal will succeed. The world certainly is more different today than it was three decades ago. Perhaps those changes will enable current experiments to succeed.

The present extended geographical parish church, or the mission Bible studies of the First Baptist Church in Arlington, Texas, are the product of two innovations: transportation and communication. Because we have telephones, computers, fax machines and various media tools to network missions, it now is possible to build a larger network of mission Sunday Schools than previously possible. The question remains: Are they products of the New Testament?

2
Sunday School
Begins with Children

Highlands Community Church
Renton, Washington

Rev. James A. Amandus, Pastor

Rev. Wallace R. Wilson,
Founding Pastor

"MY TWO-YEAR-OLD DAUGHTER CAME OUT OF SUNDAY SCHOOL laughing," Cindy Wentworth, a young mother, said in describing their first visit to the Highlands Community Church in Renton, Washington. The previous week they had visited another church and her daughter left Sunday School crying. So it was a welcome surprise when her daughter entered the car outside the Highlands church and said, "Mom, let's come back here." They have—for seven years.

The Highlands experience has not always been so joyous. Brenda Chance, the preschool departmental superintendent, remembered the little boy who cried and screamed week after week when he entered the Sunday School. "I hate Sunday School," the boy said.

That occurred before Highlands switched to Sunday School learning centers. The boy was happy with the change. His mother said he actually looked forward to attending Sunday School. "It is exciting to see a child whom you have written off turn his attitude around," Chance said. "Now he takes an active part in class."

Teachers Who Love Children

The Highlands Sunday School has many things going for it. One of the reasons, said church member Art Hoyt, is that "we have teachers who love children."

Another man said the Sunday School focus on children is the best thing about Highlands Community Church. "We have an incredibly strong children's ministry," he said, "and the increased resources we are attempting to pour into that ministry makes it a priority for the future."

The switch to a learning center approach to children's ministries also involved a curriculum change to Gospel Light's literature.

"I was not pleased with the program we used to have because we just talked (told stories) to the children and made them color pictures at a table," Chance said. "When I adapted Gospel Light curriculum to learning centers, I was able to let the kids be kids."

Influencing Children for Life

"Kids this young will formulate their ideas about Jesus, the church and the future. If you influence them as children, your ministry continues as they become youth and adults...you influence them for life.

"But more than just ministry to children, we minister to their parents as well," Chance said. "Parents want to attend where their children are happy."

Although one of her primary goals is to make children happy, another goal is learning. "Happy children learn and unhappy children learn, it is just that happy children learn the right things."

When Highlands switched to learning centers, it required a much larger staff than one teacher and assistant for each class. "Instead of being a teacher, I had to become a manager of teachers," Chance said. "Then each preschool class took a teacher and three to six helpers, depending on the size of the class."

As the classes have grown, so has the number of workers. When the switch to learning centers was made, the names of 75 children appeared on the roll. Now, the average is 210 to 230.

Church Began in a Log Cabin

The Highlands Community Church was planted by Pastor Wallace Wilson in 1948, as a product of a children's outreach camp in the area. Wallace Wilson, who is now retired, and his wife, Inez, used a log cabin, pumped their water by hand and ministered to the children in the Highlands area.

Temporary war housing had been built in the area for people who built bombers during World War II. When the war ended, the apartment complex closed and the people were expected to leave. Some did, but many returned because they liked the area.

Wallace Wilson said, "When I came to the Highlands area, there was no Sunday School, yet about 10,000 people lived in the temporary project that was soon to be dismantled."

The biggest problem facing any Sunday School in America is recruitment. Highland's philosophy is to reproduce workers rather than to recruit workers.

Wilson began a Sunday School in the community hall and gymnasium. During the week, children were visited and led to Christ. Then they were enrolled in summer camps. The work was called Highlands Community Sunday School and in 1950 was organized into a local church and incorporated by the state of Washington.

Ministry Began to Grow

About 30 adults and 300 children attended when Highlands was organized as a church. Because the work was growing, Wilson asked for help from the School of Religion at Seattle Pacific University (at that time Simpson Bible Institute). Bible school students helped give biblical direction to the work.

In the early days, the church focused primarily on children. Contests were effective in that day. "In the summertime we had a parade with the police department, the fire department and any other department that would work with us," Wilson said. "We did everything we could to attract children to Sunday School and Vacation Bible School."

After nine years of attempting to negotiate with the government to buy the property for their building, Wilson went to Senator Henry "Scoop" Jackson, who made a senatorial inquiry into the Federal Housing Administration. Within a few days the church was able to purchase 2.56 acres. The church has since purchased an additional 5 acres.

First Unit Too Small

The first unit was built in 1958 and shortly thereafter was too small. The church offered two services, and in 1962 ground was broken for a second building. Soon the church returned to dual Sunday Schools and dual worship services. Within a period of time, three church services were offered.

Beginning in 1963, the church added staff members and at one time had eight men and one woman on staff. Because of its commitment to Sunday School, the church began adding women in ministry. "The most rapidly growing part of our Sunday School was the nursery and preschool," Wilson said. "So, we looked for women to head up those programs and found Bev Jackson, an excellent teacher in the Renton School District, who did a great job in the Sunday School."

Recruit by Reproducing

Technically, the biggest problem facing any Sunday School in America is recruitment. First, teachers must be found who will volunteer to take ownership of a class. Second, when a teacher is absent for one week, a substitute must be found.

"Our philosophy is to reproduce workers rather than to recruit workers," Wilson said.

Recruiting Volunteers

At Highlands, recruitment takes several forms. Much of it is done personally. Chance, for example, telephoned a public school teacher of special education and asked her to think about helping in the children's Sunday School class. She also asked the teacher, "Will you pray about it?"

"Sure I will," the teacher responded.

The next September the special education teacher was rather reluctant, but she became one of the best teachers in the department. The following fall she volunteered to work on an administration level.

On another occasion, Janine Hoyt, a high school girl, came and said she wanted to teach. Brenda was skeptical, "I didn't know how to respond to her, so we met and we talked over a few things. She said she was ready, so she comes prepared every Sunday. As a matter of fact, I think she's better prepared than some of our adult teachers. She is excited and I have complete confidence in her."

While Janine was used on a learning team of teachers, she would never go in and take a class by herself. But she goes in and takes control of the situation. She has her schedule and tells everybody what she is going to do, and how they will respond. She hands a schedule to everyone and is always well prepared. Even though Janine is a high schooler, Brenda says, "I can trust her." When she asks the whole class to be quiet for prayer, they respond.

Since July 1992, Janine along with the rest of her family, are now serving as career missionaries in the Philippines. In her last letter, Janine shared that she and her sister are involved in outreach to Filipino children. She also acknowledged that her preschool training at Highlands Community Church is invaluable.

Drawing from the Awana Pool

For church workers, Highlands dips into Awana, a children's Bible-based activity program similar to the Boy Scouts.

Several years ago the church sponsored Boys Brigade and Pioneer Girls, each of which had approximately 50 pupils. But when the programs did not seem to meet the needs of the church, the switch was made to Awana.

Today, approximately 500 are enrolled in the program that features the excitement of games, Scripture memory and development of children.

Secret Weapon Unveiled

The church believes that its secret weapon is developing staff through the Awana program. It is easy to recruit Awana workers because they see the weekly reinforcement of learning verses and weekly progress. Previously, the church had approximately 19 leaders working with Boys Brigade and Pioneer Girls. Today, more than 100 leaders work in Awana.

The Awana introductory program of Cubbies works with children, most of whom cannot read. After their parents hear their verses and sign the Cubbie book, the parents often become involved as leaders.

Reliable Leaders Sought

The church does some recruitment through public announcements. Of course, most churches use this approach, but the leadership of Highlands is looking for reliable, committed people who say, "Yes, I will show up," and then show up.

In the fall of 1991, the church did not have enough teachers for the first-grade Sunday School program. So it was cancelled for three weeks. A letter was written to the parents telling them that until teachers were recruited, classes would not be in session for their children. Immediately, three women volunteered to teach the girls and a couple of men came forward to teach the boys.

Although some church members opposed cancelling the first-grade Sunday School, Chance said, "I think part of the recruitment umbrella is that when you make a statement that there are going to be three children to one adult in the learning center, we need to stick with it."

No Baby-sitting, Please

When they did not have a preschool teacher, someone walked in and said, "I will go in with the kids." Brenda said, "No, you won't."

Brenda insisted that a teacher must be prepared. "I do not want baby-sitting, and we do not have baby-sitting." She went on to explain that if they had given in to the heat of that moment, they would still have a philosophy of baby-sitting.

People may believe that someone else will do it, but that is not always the case. Highlands has another approach to recruitment. If children attend Sunday School, parents are required to work in Sunday School (or some place else in the church). As a result, even though there is a strong outreach program to needy areas, the church expects the parents of those families who come to Highlands to work with children there.

"The reason we want parents working in Sunday School is to focus on the total family," Chance said. "We're not here to provide religious education just for kids. We're here to assist the family in providing religious education for the parents and their kids."

Men in Every Classroom

"I have made it a practice to have a man in every one of the classrooms," Chance said. "Men bring a different tone to the classroom and make a big difference. As an illustration, children from a single mother's home just cling to the male teacher."

The men are not just in the background as a male image. They sit and talk with the children and have a willing attitude to teach.

A Place for Men, Too

Becky and Mike Mayer taught in the learning center as a husband and wife team, although Mike spent most of his time in the background. Becky, who was the more outgoing of the two, was the teacher and Mike was the helper. When the church needed a first-grade teacher, however, Mike volunteered to be the lead teacher for first-grade boys. He asked to teach with another man, all of which was a surprise to Becky.

When they returned home from church, Mike told her that he had volunteered to take on a class by himself. Becky offered to help, but he said he was confident that he could handle the assignment alone. Now, he and his high-school son, Robbie, lead an exciting class.

Children Love Male Contacts

"Kids like to sit on their laps, hug them, and men communicate so much through touch," Chance said. "It seems like it takes a longer time for a man to say that he will teach, but once a commitment is made, they do a super job."

She cited several reasons why men are reluctant to teach children. First, there is the initial hesitation that it is a demeaning job. Second is the false expectation that Sunday School teaching is a woman's job. Then, sometimes men have a fear of or feel uncomfortable around small children. Despite all this, men have become outstanding teachers of children at Highlands Community Church.

When a Child Misbehaves

When a "problem child" is found in the Sunday School, the parents are invited to meet with the teachers to talk about the problem. Often, Sunday School teachers find parents saying things such as, "I just don't know what to do with this kid."

This situation offers an excellent opportunity for spiritual ministry to the parents. The answer is not always punitive discipline; it often may be corrective discipline and direction for the parents as well as for the child.

Chance said a disruptive child is sent to the superintendent's office. There the child is counseled and dealt with appropriately. If the misbehavior happens again, the superintendent meets with the parents.

Some Are Asked to Leave

If the parents are uncooperative, the church asks the child not to

According to the Gallup Poll, the young adults, ages 18-35, comprise the fastest-growing segment of the American church population.

return to class without a parent being present for the entirety of the class. When parents are uncooperative, they are told, "We are sorry, but we cannot permit the child to remain in Sunday School."

No one at the Sunday School would physically touch a child by corporal punishment. On a few occasions, when a mother has been called to deal with a child, the mother has spanked her child. As a result, when the child sees a mother coming, it's an effective way to solve a problem.

Conclusion

According to the Gallup Poll, the young adults, ages 18-35, comprise the fastest-growing segment of the American church population. However, many of those young adults will not remain in a church that does not have a program they feel is adequate for their children.

Analysts are not sure if young adults attend church because of their children or if they come because of the unique need that arises because they have children. Whatever the motive, it is clear that a church must have a vibrant program to teach children if the church wants to reach their parents.

Ministry Application

A BLUEPRINT FOR BEGINNING TEACHING CENTERS

The following points are offered as sequential steps for introducing teaching centers into a Bible school. Local conditions will dictate whether the steps may be followed completely or modified in some details.

1. Study available material and literature about teaching centers.
2. Evaluate your Sunday School to determine whether or not teaching centers will help you become more effective.

    a. Is there adequate room space?
    b. What extra equipment is needed?

    c. Will changes be needed in the organization of the Sunday School to accommodate a team approach?

    d. Is leadership available and trained to introduce and establish a successful teaching approach in your Sunday School?

    e. Will the present curriculum be adaptable to a teaching center approach?

3. Agree on the objectives to be accomplished.
4. Study the kinds of team organizations (hierarchical, democratic, etc.) and choose the one that will best suit your needs.
5. Don't introduce teaching centers until there is a full set of teachers (lead teacher, regular teachers, resource teacher, clerical aid, etc.).
6. Begin with one level at a time. If your Sunday School is departmentally graded, begin with a department. If the departments are crowded, choose one grade of the department to begin with. For example, choose the first grade if the Primary Department is crowded.
7. Choose the team personnel on the basis of their qualifications and training.
8. Choose the lead teacher at the beginning. He/she should have both good leadership ability and the ability to train others to teach children. (Some would recommend choosing a leader before choosing team personnel.)
9. Give the team in-service training with the age with which they will be working. If possible, have them observe a neighboring church where the concept is being carried on.
10. Plan, organize and coordinate the curriculum for teaching centers.
11. If you are planning for children, divide the assigned Sun-

day School room into activity sections (not content sections). This should be done by the team. Space should be provided for a worship center, a resource center, an activity center, a nature center, and of course, places for small-group work.

12. Prior to the inauguration of teaching centers, the following items should be considered for good public relations:

   a. A time of orientation for parents;
   b. A time of orientation for pupils involved in the program;
   c. A time of orientation for the rest of the staff to the nature and aims of team teaching.

13. Secure the materials needed for the resource centers.
14. Determine the criteria by which the pupils will be grouped into small units for instruction.
15. Establish a time for a weekly teachers' planning session.
16. Design a flexible schedule, creating blocks of time for largegroup activities (worship, stories, singing, etc.), blocks of time for small-group activities (group instruction, handwork activities, workbook projects, etc.) and blocks of time for individual pupil activities apart from the groups (library time, presession activities, playing, etc.).
17. Begin.

Beginning teaching centers is like any other adventure in the church. It requires faith, vision and boldness. Faith is needed to trust God to work through the new activity approach to teaching in the lives of teachers and pupils. Vision is needed to see the advantages such a program can provide to the pupils and to your church. Finally, boldness is needed.

A PLAN FOR TEACHING CENTERS

	LEAD TEACHER	TEACHER A	TEACHER B	TEACHER C
As the children arrive.	Visits with any parents who come and advises them about the time of dismissal. Last minute preparations for storytelling.	Writes name tags.	Shows groups of children around the room when they are tagged.	Helps teacher A when needed. Puts up charts. Arranges chairs in story circle. Sounds chord for gathering, or taps a bell.
Introductions. **Storytelling.**	Introduces teaching team and children. Tells the Bible story with the use of visuals.	Sits with 8 to 10 children in circle.	The same as Teacher A.	Plays soft music as children move to story circle.
Discussion of plans with group.	Leads the discussion.	Takes part as a member of the group and enters into discussion.		
Playing games.	Helps with games. Readies material for working on projects.	Leads games.	Prepares work table.	Plays music for game.
Working on projects.	Works with one group on project Directs cleanup.	Works with another group. Helps with cleanup.	Work with another group. Helps with cleanup.	Helps with one of the groups. Chords (or bell) and music.
Planning for next week. If leaders are alternating, choose next weeks leader.	A member of the group.	A member of the group.	A member of the group.	Arranges worship center. Plays softly to introduce worship.
Closing worship.	Leads worship.	Leads reading of Scripture.	Leads singing.	Plays for songs.
Evaluation.	When the children have left, the teaching team briefly reviews the session, and decides how to strengthen weak points before the next session. Team assigns specific responsibilities; makes out Team Teaching Chart for the next session; commits the day's efforts to God.			

3
A Purpose-driven Sunday School

Saddleback Valley Community Church
Mission Viejo, California

Rev. Rick Warren, Pastor

𝒲HERE DID SADDLEBACK VALLEY COMMUNITY CHURCH, THIS dynamic church of 6,000, originate?

Did it begin when Rick Warren met in the home of Don Dale for Bible study with seven people in January 1980?

Did it begin when Warren rented facilities for the first church service on Easter 1980?

Did it begin when Warren, as a student at Southwestern Baptist Theological Seminary, searched the library for every book he could find on church growth and read all 72 of them?

Or did it begin when Warren walked the streets, knocked on doors and asked questions in Orange County, California? (See questions in ministry application at the end of this chapter.)

Armed with a Vision

Warren is a fourth-generation Southern Baptist pastor whose great-grandfather was converted under Dr. Charles Spurgeon. Armed with a vision of starting a church, Warren moved to the Greater Los Angeles area in January 1980 with his wife, Kay, and their four-month-old daughter, Amy.

They arrived with their belongings packed in a U-Haul trailer during the rush-hour gridlock of Southern California traffic. Because Warren did not know anyone, he found a real estate office in Orange County and met Don Dale.

Here to Start a Church

"I am here to start a church," the church planter said. "I need a place to live and I don't have any money!"

Within two hours, Dale found a condominium for the Warren family that was rent-free during the first month. The following Friday, the Dale and Warren families met for Bible study at what was to become Saddleback Valley Community Church in Mission Viejo.

Running on the Fast Track

Now, church attendance averages 6,000, and more than 15,000 attended the twelfth anniversary of the church on Easter Sunday 1992. Saddleback has been listed as the twelfth fastest-growing church in America by *Church Growth Today* magazine.

That growth is unusual because the church is located within driving distance of such outstanding pastors as Robert Schuller at Crystal Cathedral, Chuck Smith at Calvary Chapel of Costa Mesa and Charles Swindoll of the Evangelical Free Church in Fullerton.

When Warren was going door-to-door asking why people did not attend church, he identified four reasons:

- First, people said sermons were boring and were not relevant to their lives.
- Second, churches were unfriendly to visitors.
- Third, churches were more interested in money than in people.
- Fourth, churches did not provide quality child care.

Develops Seeker Sensitive Church

Warren developed a four-fold strategy to answer the objections of the Orange County residents and to attract them to what he calls a "seeker sensitive" church:

- Quality child care is necessary to attract young families.
- He preaches humorous sermons that are practical to their lives and solve their problems. The sermons are based on Bible answers.

- He has organized the church to be friendly. He tells people to "shake hands with 75 people."
- He makes it known that visitors are never asked to contribute financially but are asked to fill out cards to receive a free tape of the service.

Because Warren had a double zeal—first as a missionary to win souls and second as a marketing expert—he knew he would have to develop a profile for his target audience. He coined the phrase "Saddleback Sam" to describe a typical resident he was trying to reach.

Meet Saddleback Sam

Saddleback Sam had several characteristics. He believed in God but did not attend church. He made good money but did not make enough to acquire everything he desired. He is a nice guy but is stressed out and is searching for answers in life.

The church is affiliated with the Southern Baptist Convention, but Warren did not use the word "Baptist" in the title because in California many people thought that it would be a "Southern-cultured church."

Many Southern Californian's believe that Baptists only preach against things. As a result of not using the name Baptist, the Saddleback Church has a large representation of Roman Catholics, mainline denominational members and people who have never been members of any church. The church attracts people of all ages but a majority are baby boomers (i.e., people born between 1946 and 1964).

Sport Shirts, Reeboks and Blue Jeans

The church service features the heavy boom of contemporary rock music but lyrics that are decidedly Christian. The people sing, sway and clap their hands to the rhythmic music. It is obvious that they enjoy themselves at Saddleback. Also, the audience comes to church on Sunday morning laid back and comfortable in sports shirts, Reeboks and blue jeans. Warren seldom wears a coat and is often without a tie.

The church owns no facilities and meets in rented public school auditoriums. In 13 years, the church has used 57 different buildings. Baptisms are performed in swimming pools or whirlpools, coined by Warren as "jacuzzis for Jesus." More than 70 percent of the members of Saddleback were converted and baptized at the church. Saddleback has grown largely through conversions rather than through transfers.

Sunday School Pilgrimage

Church attendance grew to 200 during the first year. "I felt I was running an orphanage because everyone in the church was a new Christian," Warren said. Because the new church lacked strong leadership, Sunday School was not offered.

In about 1983, three years after the church was founded, Warren asked, "Why don't we give a standard Sunday School our best shot?" If North Phoenix (Arizona) Baptist Church could attract nearly 7,000 people, he thought a similar target was feasible in California.

Program Based on Growth Goals
Warren used the Southern Baptist Growth Spiral program, which was built on setting growth goals. He also began teaching the Sunday School lesson to the teachers each week, simply because the new believers needed help in learning content and in preparing lessons. In addition, he conducted Sunday School retreats, conferences and brought in specialists to train the workers.

However, Sunday School attendance remained at 300 while the church attendance jumped from 500 to 750 to 1,000 to 1,500 and then to 2,000.

The problem of attracting people to Sunday School was sociological, not theological. People in Saddleback's area had money, and money meant options.

··

The problem of attracting people to Sunday School was sociological, not theological, Warren said. "I discovered that people in our area had money, and money meant options."

Audience Wanted Options
He realized that Southern Californians were balking over the traditional Sunday School in which everyone studies the same thing at the same place at the same time. Warren discovered they wanted options in four areas: time, service, curriculum and methods of learning.

As a result, the pastor changed the Sunday School program from a fixed curriculum to an elective type that allowed every Sunday School class or teacher to choose a topic. He told teachers he did not care when classes studied the Bible so long as they studied the Bible sometime during the week.

Teachers also were not required to use the Southern Baptist Sunday School curriculum but were given a list of approved curricula to choose cafeteria style. The church printed a brochure listing the classes by affinity groups, stages of life or interests. Each listing of a class emphasized the qualifications of the teacher.

Hands-off Approach Unsuccessful

Originally, attendance exploded, but eventually, attendance began to decline. "I knew I was on to something as far as giving people options," Warren said, "but I realized a total hands-off approach of our staff was not working."

Warren examined a number of successful small groups, including those conducted by Dale Galloway at New Life Community Church in Portland, Oregon.

Meanwhile, he visited one of the largest Southern Baptist churches with one of the most expensive Sunday School facilities and came away discouraged. He did not want to spend millions of dollars for a building that would only be used one hour each week.

Sunday Schools in the Homes

Warren decided it was better stewardship to use the homes of members. He wanted to use homes because they are geographically expandable. He felt the use of homes for adult Sunday Schools represented good stewardship of money and would promote fellowship.

"If you put a man in a Sunday School class and stand a teacher in front of him, he will probably clam up and not say a word all morning," Warren said. "Place the same man on a couch on Friday evening without his coat and tie, with a cup of coffee in his hands, and he will 'talk his head off.'" At that point, the small groups in Saddleback Valley Community Church began to grow.

The church offers five types of small groups based on the five purposes of the church: worship, evangelism, edification, fellowship and ministry. Each group specializes and emphasizes one purpose. This offers people options.

A Place for Children, Too
Approximately 1,400 children attend Sunday Schools that are held simultaneously with three Sunday morning worship services and one Saturday night service.

Several different curricula, based on the purpose of each class, are used. In grades 6 to 12, a "rally type" approach is used, and the church writes the curriculum.

The church has only a few adult Sunday School classes that Warren calls "token classes for the traditionalist." Even though attendance is limited, the church believes that type of Sunday School meets the needs of some people.

Warren has developed a Sunday School program that builds on knowledge, perspective, conviction, character and skills. The goal is to produce "doers of the word, and not hearers only."

Whereas most churches develop a Sunday School program that progresses lesson by lesson, Warren has developed one that builds upon five objectives: knowledge, perspective, conviction, character and skills. The goal is to produce "doers of the word, and not hearers only" (Jas. 1:22).

Sunday School as a Strategy
"Sunday School is a strategy," Warren said. "Sunday School is not a program." He points to Arthur Flake, who was the architect of the Southern Baptist Sunday School system. Warren said Flake's growth principles apply to a church but not necessarily

on Sunday morning and to small groups.

The foundation for growth of Warren's church has occurred first in the small-group program that gives pastoral care to people and second in the CLASS program that produces maturity in people.

The baseball diamond best reflects Saddleback's strategy of equipping people for their Christian life and service. Just as a person must go from first base to second, and third before arriving at home; so they must go from Class 101 to 201 and then 301 before arriving at the completion of their training process.

"When I first started the church, I tried to get everyone to make a deep, complete commitment to Christ at the membership class," Warren said.

"For example, I wanted them to make a commitment to church membership, to ministry, to witnessing and to separation from sin. I found that approach didn't work in Southern California. I had to learn to lead people by steps—one step at a time. People must be led gradually to increase their commitment."

Four classes are offered as a person moves through five levels of commitment.

Commitment and membership are achieved in CLASS 101, "Discovering Saddleback Membership," which is taught every month. More than 450 were enrolled in the class during November 1992, a Saddleback record.

CLASS 201, "Discovering Spiritual Maturity," addresses habits of life that are necessary for spiritual growth. CLASS 301, "Discovering My Ministry," helps members discover their place in service.

"Discovering My Mission," CLASS 401, is offered as a member moves into a covenant level that involves a commitment to share the good news with other people through church missions opportunities.

"Typically, most churches get stuck into teaching content,

never teaching skills and maturity," Warren said and pointed out that Saddleback's purpose-driven strategy is explained and symbolized by two diagrams: five concentric circles and a baseball diamond. (The diagrams appear in the **Ministry Application** section.)

Five Circles of Commitment

The Five Circles of Commitment represent the strategy that pastor Warren uses in moving a person from his/her first visit to the church to maturity and service.

Fifth Circle—The Community: "The community is the uncommitted and nonattenders we want to reach for Jesus Christ," Warren said. "We target our ministry to the 'Saddleback Sams and Samanthas.' More specifically, we consider the community as anyone who attends at least 4 times a year, that is, Easter, Christmas, Mother's Day and one other occasion." Approximately 18,000 attended at least 4 times in 1992.

Fourth Circle—The Crowd: Warren describes the fourth group as the 5,000 to 7,000 regular Sunday morning attenders. The strategy is to move casual attendees to a commitment membership. Many in the crowd are not believers.

Third Circle—The Congregation: The church has approximately 3,000 adults who have attended the membership class and have signed the covenant. (A copy of the covenant appears in the Ministry Application section.)

Second Circle—Committed to Maturity: Warren calls those in the second circle good people who are committed to becoming godly. An estimated 2,400 people in this group are people who love the Lord but for some reason have not yet found a ministry. To reach this level, a person must commit to 3 basic habits and must sign a covenant that involves time, money and relationships. (A copy appears in the Ministry Application section.) The person must commit to a daily quiet time with God, a weekly tithe to God and to be a part of a small group.

The Inner Circle—The Core-Committed: Warren estimates 1,000 people are core members. They are identifiable lay-ministers involved in nearly 70 ministries. Two people handle job placement. The people in the core ministry have completed the 4 basic classes of the baseball diamond to develop skills and maturity and have signed a ministry covenant. (A copy appears in Ministry Application section.)

People in Each Circle Targeted

"We believe you need a specific strategy to meet the spiritual needs of those in each circle and help move them closer to God," Warren said.

"Our strategy is to get the community into the crowd; that means we must get them attending every week. We preach practical sermons directed toward their needs, and contemporary music is provided." The entire service is designed to move people from being spectators to participants.

The church then seeks to move the crowd into the congregation and to become committed to Christ and His Church. "The difference between an attender and a member is commitment," Warren said. "It's like the difference between a man and woman just living together and their actually getting married.

"Everything we do at Saddleback is aimed at moving people through the circles of commitment to get every person into the core where they have a ministry in the church and a mission in the world."

Sunday School Without Walls

As a result, Warren developed a teaching program he calls, "A Sunday School Without Walls." He also describes it as a Sunday

School that graduates people when they complete the curriculum called "CLASS."

More than an Attendance Pin

"Typically, most adults in Sunday School get stuck in one class and just study one quarterly after another," Warren said. "A guy can go to Sunday School for years and the most he gets out of it is maybe an attendance pin."

At Saddleback Valley Community Church, people move through four levels, advancing only after they have completed a previous level.

"A church is defined by what it is committed to do," Warren said, "and our adult Sunday School is committed to moving our people into membership, then maturity, then ministry, then mission."

Church Built Through Purpose

Warren believes that a church must be built through purpose. Saddleback draws its purposes from two key Scriptures: The Great Commandment (Matthew 22:36-40) and The Great Commission (Matthew 28:19,20).

SADDLEBACK'S SLOGAN:

"A Great Commitment to the Great Commandment and the Great Commission will grow a Great Church."

"My goal at Saddleback is to build the most spiritually mature church in the nation by the year 2000," Warren said. While some people believe that might be an auspicious goal, he said the new Sunday School programs were developed to lead to that goal.

"We believe the shoe must never tell the foot how big it

should grow," Warren said. "We've never let the lack of a building stop us from growing. But after using 57 different buildings in our history, we laugh and say, 'This is the church where, if you can figure out where we are this week, you get to come.'"

Ministry Application

SADDLEBACK
5 CIRCLES OF COMMITMENT

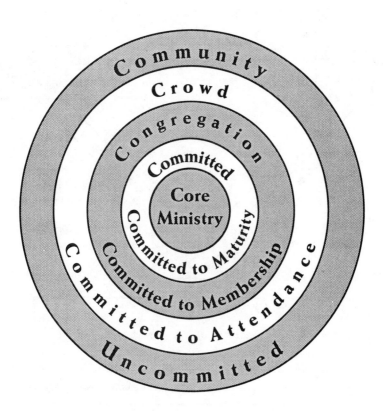

SADDLEBACK'S PROGRAM TO HELP YOU GROW THROUGH CHRISTIAN LIFE AND SERVICE SEMINARS

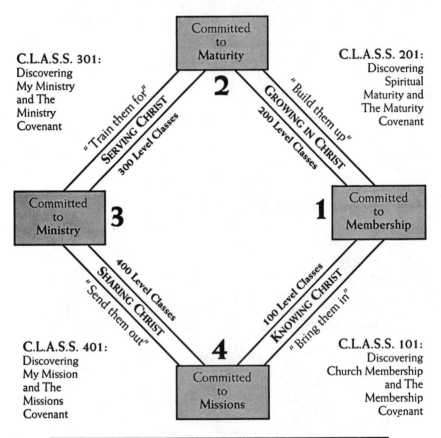

C.L.A.S.S. 301:
Discovering
My Ministry
and The
Ministry
Covenant

C.L.A.S.S. 201:
Discovering
Spiritual
Maturity and
The Maturity
Covenant

Committed to Maturity **2**

"Train them for" SERVING CHRIST
300 Level Classes

"Build them up" GROWING IN CHRIST
200 Level Classes

Committed to Ministry **3**

Committed to Membership **1**

400 Level Classes SHARING CHRIST "Send them out"

100 Level Classes KNOWING CHRIST "Bring them in"

Committed to Missions **4**

C.L.A.S.S. 401:
Discovering
My Mission
and The
Missions
Covenant

C.L.A.S.S. 101:
Discovering
Church Membership
and The
Membership
Covenant

AN OVERVIEW OF C.L.A.S.S.

100 Level Seminars:	To lead people to Christ and **membership** at Saddleback
200 Level Seminars:	To grow people to spiritual **maturity**
300 Level Seminars:	To equip people with the skills they need for **ministry**
400 Level Seminars:	To enlist people to the worldwide **mission** of sharing Christ

C.L.A.S.S. #201
SPIRITUAL MATURITY COVENANT CARD

MY 1991 GROWTH COVENANT

I Commit to:

☐ A DAILY TIME WITH GOD ....MARK 1:35
Personal Bible Reading and Prayer.

☐ A WEEKLY TITHE TO GOD ....1 COR. 16:2
Giving the first 10% of my income.

☐ A COMMITTED TEAM FOR GOD HEB.10:25
Fellowship with believers in a small group.

_____   _____
　　　Signature　　　　　　　　　Pastor

(FRONT)

"Take the time and trouble to keep yourself spiritual-ly fit. Bodily fitness has a limited value, but spiritual fitness is of unlimited value, for it holds promise both for this present life and for the life to come."
1 Tim. 4:7(ph)

Address:_____

_____

_____

(BACK)

C.L.A.S.S. #301
MINISTRY COVENANT CARD

MY MINISTRY COVENANT

Having committed myself to membership and the habits essential for spiritual maturity, and agreeing with Saddleback's Ministry Statement, I commit to...

- Discover my unique *shape* for ministry and serve in the area that best expresses what God made me to be.
- Prepare for ministry by participating in S.A.L.T. and C.L.A.S.S.
- Demonstrate a servant's heart by serving in secondary ministries as the Body needs me.
- Cooperate with other ministries and place the greater good of the whole Body over the needs of my ministry.

_____   _____
signed   date

(FRONT)

This certifies that_____
is a commissioned minister of Jesus Christ through the Saddleback Valley Community Church and is entrusted with the related responsibilities and privileges.

_____
Rick Warren, Pastor

(BACK)

THE SADDLEBACK VISION

It is the dream *of a place where the hurting, the hopeless, the discouraged, the depressed, the frustrated and confused can find love, acceptance, help, hope, forgiveness, guidance and encouragement.*

It is the dream *of sharing the Good News of Jesus Christ with the hundreds of thousands of residents in south Orange County.*

It is the dream *of 20,000 members growing together in spiritual maturity through Bible studies, seminars, retreats, and fellowship—loving, laughing, and learning together, understanding God's wonderful plan and living life to its greatest potential.*

It is the dream *of sending out hundreds of career missionaries and church workers all around the world, and sending out our members by the thousands on short term mission projects to every continent. It is the dream of starting at least one new daughter church a year.*

It is the dream *of 50 acres of land, on which will be built a regional church for southern Orange County—with beautiful yet efficient facilities...including a worship center seating thousands, counseling and prayer center, classrooms for Bible study and training lay ministers, and a professional aerobics recreational center. All of this will be designed to minister to the total person—spiritually, emotionally, physically and socially—and set in a peaceful, inspiring garden setting with bright flowers, beautiful trees, and pools of still water, sparkling fountains, and flowing streams. I stand before you today and state in confident assurance that these dreams will be realized. Why?*

BECAUSE THEY ARE INSPIRED BY GOD!

From Pastor Rick's First Sermon
March 30, 1980

NEIGHBORHOOD SURVEY OF THE UNCHURCHED*

Saddleback Questionnaire

Rick Warren's Five Questions:

1. Are you an active member of a nearby church? (If the answer is yes, the interview stops there. Wish the person well, but you are looking for opinion of the "unchurched.")
2. What do you think is the greatest need in (insert the name of your community)?
3. Why do you think most people don't attend church? (Be sure you don't change the wording of this key question.)
4. If you were looking for a church in the area, what kinds of things would you look for?
5. What advice would you give me as the pastor of a nearby church? What, for example, could I do for you?

Take notes as you talk, then leave the person a brochure describing your church. When you have 100 pages of notes, study them for a long time in an attitude of prayer. You should find you have a good handle on the felt needs of the unchurched in your area.

*These five questions were adapted from questions that Robert Schuller used years ago. This information is extracted from the book, *Leading Your Church to Growth* by C. Peter Wagner, Regal Books, 1984.

4
A Return to Sunday School Enrollment

Florence Baptist Temple
Florence, South Carolina

Rev. Bill Monroe, Pastor

$\mathcal{B}$ILL MONROE WAS LEADING MUSIC IN A CHURCH IN INDIANAPOLIS, Indiana, during the late 1960s when he read this author's book, *The Ten Largest Sunday Schools and What Makes Them Grow.* The book gave him a vision of a great Sunday School and stretched his faith to plant one. He thought of his home state of South Carolina, realizing he did not know of a great Sunday School or a great church anywhere in that state.

During the Sunday morning gospel invitation at his Indianapolis church, 12 people had come forward to receive Christ. He thought, *I don't know of a single church in South Carolina that has this many getting saved every Sunday.* He resigned from his job and moved his family to South Carolina to begin a church.

In Search of a Great Church

A friend told him that Florence, South Carolina, needed a great church. Late in 1969 he went to Florence, a city of 32,000, rented an abandoned theater building at the local airport for $58.50 a month and began contacting people to come to his Sunday School.

He was certain that God had led him, but while preparing for his first worship service, he realized he had never preached a sermon in his life.

"I had taught Sunday School on many occasions," he later recalled. "So I just prepared a Sunday School lesson and shouted it!"

A Leaky Roof
Florence Baptist Temple was a reality even though the roof to the building leaked. At one time during a hard rain, the roof sprang a leak, drenching Monroe with water. Rain also was

responsible for cancelled church services several times during the next two years.

"No one took his coat off that first winter," Monroe recalled. "Two hundred dollars a month spent on fuel oil couldn't keep the building warm. Sunday School was held in a room out back, which was nothing more than tin wrapped around studs in a concrete floor. Women stuffed rags in the holes in the nursery wall to keep it warm and had to watch the children carefully to prevent them from ripping decaying beaver board off the walls."

In March 1970, Monroe enjoyed one of his greatest victories. The congregation prayed for 55 people to come to Sunday School. Gifts were given to everyone who came. Fifty-five attended.

In May, the goal was 100. As incentives, goldfish were offered as gifts and a local quartet performed. The result: 102 came to Sunday School.

Two Hundred Attend First Anniversary

On the church's first anniversary in November, attendance reached 200 for the first time. The young church, with its youthful pastor, was on the march. Still the church had no capital assets but was paying the pastor a full-time salary. Monroe signed a note at the bank for $1,100 and bought 3 used buses. Sunday School attendance pushed its way to 140.

During a citywide search for property, Monroe located a 10-acre tract on Highway 301. He asked a tenant farmer for information about the property. The man went inside to phone the owner, during which time Monroe stood on the porch out of the rain, praying for God's will. They agreed on $50,000 for the land, but the church only had a $1,000 building fund. Immediately, the church sold $200,000 in bonds.

Because Monroe had built a solid foundation in the theater

building, enough income was generated to pay the bonds as they came due. The small congregation that had no material assets, then needed to buy everything:

Building and Interest	$131,800
Land	50,000
Hard Top	5,000
Driveway and Parking Lots	5,000
Illuminated Sign	2,200
Printing Press and Equipment	1,500
Office Equipment	1,500
School Desks and Chalkboards	2,000
	$199,000

The congregation moved into 15,000 square feet of new facilities on April 9, 1972, and the church had room for expansion. The new auditorium would seat 300, and the 8 classrooms furnished space for the Sunday School when the building was occupied. Monroe believes that move represented a great victory because 32 people joined the church.

Attendance Grows to 1,200

By 1980, Sunday School attendance reached 1,200. The Sunday School bus had 700 riders. Between 1980 and 1985, however, Sunday School attendance plateaued at about 1,200. He taught all the adults in one large auditorium Bible class.

Monroe thought that dividing the large class into smaller adult classes was the way to growth. So in September 1984, Monroe brought all of his deacons together, asked several of them to teach an adult Sunday School class and eliminated his large auditorium Bible class. He felt that if each of these classes would grow, perhaps doubling in attendance, the Sunday School would continue to grow.

Poor Training, Poor Attendance

However, within a few weeks problems developed. "Poor teaching was driving people away at a faster rate than good outreach could bring them in," Monroe said. Many of the deacons were not trained to teach and had no real strategy in their Sunday School classes.

Monroe cancelled most of the classes and brought the adults back into the auditorium and resumed the pastor's Bible class. The Sunday School continued the Senior Saints class of 40 people, the Young Married Class of 60 people and the Women's Bible Class of 15 women.

Monroe knew about the success of the Southern Baptist Convention's Sunday School enrollment plan. They emphasized small, adult Bible classes of approximately 10 in atten-

Monroe believes that Sunday School enrollment is the entry door to the church. Enrollment means that people have given the church permission to minister to them.

dance with a strong commitment to enrolling prospects in the class as the first step of evangelism. Monroe realized that his Sunday School roll was nothing more than names in a book. He also knew that Southern Baptists taught that Sunday School attendance will equal 40 percent of enrollment. So to build a Sunday School, he decided that if enrollment is increased, attendance will follow.

Sunday School Keyed to Enrollment

In 1988, Leon Kilbreth, a Southern Baptist evangelist, preached a Sunday School revival at the Florence Baptist Temple. That event was a turning point in the Sunday School strategy and outreach. Because of an ice storm, crowds were small, and Kilbreth had time to train Monroe and the staff with a new philosophy of Sunday School enrollment.

Now Monroe believes that Sunday School enrollment is the entry door to the church. This does not mean that every person enrolled in Sunday School is converted or has joined the church. "To me, enrollment means that people have given the church permission to minister to them," Monroe said.

Formerly Driven by Decisions

"In the old days, we were driven by decisions, and we would do anything to get a crowd," Monroe explained. "A church worker went to the front door and asked the person to make a decision for Christ. If that person said no, we had no fallback position to make a second attempt and probably never reached that person again. It seemed as though decisions governed everything we did."

Monroe envisions evangelism as a conveyor belt that moves people from one pool to another: from prospects enrolled in Sunday School, to making a profession for Christ, to being baptized, to being church members, to being trained for service.

"We continue our process of discipleship to get all attenders serving and reproducing for Christ," Monroe said. Today, 1,400 attend the Florence Baptist Temple Sunday School.

Moving from Prospect to Enrollment

Monroe defines ministry as "moving people from the prospect

file to enrollment, to membership and on to discipleship." He realizes that some of his former friends are uncomfortable with his strategy because the church cannot point to as large a number of decisions for Christ on visitation.

"My ministry is much broader than decision making, even though it represents getting people to make decisions," said Monroe, who is concerned that he remains true to the fundamentals of the Word of God and true to evangelistic outreach. "Our prospects plus our enrollment equal our ministry."

The church is still running approximately 1,400 in Sunday School, the same as 13 years ago. However, the adult attendance has more than doubled. The church no longer is a busing church; only 100 still come on buses. When the church operated a fleet of buses, the average offering was around $15,000 a week, which equals $10 per capita giving (per capita is measured by dividing attendance into total offering). Today, the church is receiving an average of $37,000 a week or about $26 per capita giving.

Conclusion

As Monroe looks at his present strategy, he believes Sunday School enrollment is the foundation for future growth. He observed that the great Baptist churches in the South that excel in evangelism are weak in disciple making. They often have many people who come in the front door but they go out the back door.

Monroe believes we could turn around the Sunday School if American churches would return to an emphasis on Sunday School enrollment with the strategy of bonding prospects to the church.

"The most important student in Sunday School is the enrolled student who does not attend," Monroe said. By enrolling, "This student has told me he wants to follow Christ, he wants me to minister to him and I have a good possibility of bringing him into New Testament discipleship."

Ministry Application

Sunday School Enrollment Orientation

When Sunday Schools were healthier, there was the unseen foundation of Sunday School enrollment. Enrollment refers to a pupil's name being recorded in the roll book, and that he/she has joined the class. But this is more than placing a name on a list. The strategy of enrollment emphasizes belonging to the class, being accepted by other pupils and the teacher giving spiritual watchcare over the pupil.

When Sunday School enrollment was emphasized properly, members had a deeper loyalty to the class because of accountability and responsibility. When a member on the roll was absent, teachers felt responsible to contact them with a view of getting them back into regular attendance.

Sunday School enrollment meant submembership by which prospects could identify with a church, yet not be a member. There was a time when a businessman might join the men's Bible class at the local Presbyterian church, yet not be able to fulfill the doctrinal requirements. At another place someone might join a Bible class because that person was saved, yet not be able to meet the life-style requirements of the church. In some obvious situations, unsaved people have joined Sunday School when they were unable to join the church.

Why Enrollment Declined

Sunday School enrollment had declined because some leaders wanted to emphasize the credibility of actual attendance rather than to count names on a roll. Perhaps they felt that enrollment was a falsely bloated measure of quality.

Because many people on the attendance rolls don't attend regularly, some might have felt it was spiritually dishonest to measure a Sunday School by its roll. As a result, church leaders lost interest in enrollment and it declined.

Some people felt enrollment was an American plan that emphasized a program as a way to keep up attendance. In a wrongly conceived plan to return to what was thought to be biblical Christianity, they de-emphasized enrollment.

Some people also felt that Sunday School enrollment created a false sense of salvation. It was suggested that when unsaved people belonged to the Sunday School, they might mistakenly think they belonged to Christ. Therefore, enrollment was eliminated.

Still others wanted to emphasize the credibility of actual attendance, not unseen people on a roll. As a result, in the late 1960s many Sunday Schools began reporting only attendance figures. At the same time, most denominations stopped gathering Sunday School enrollment figures.

What was not emphasized by the denomination or local churches soon began to fade. Sunday Schools stopped giving attention to the roll. Enrollment lost its meaning, and those names on the roll basically supplied a mailing and attendance list.

What Happened During Decline

First, during the decline, the Sunday School began to take less responsibility for the spiritual care of its members. Because the names on the roll did not refer to people who should be in attendance, teachers tended to stop mailing postcards to absentees, or phoning those who were absent or visiting members who were ill.

Second, the Sunday School emphasized stronger academic orientation. This is a flip side to the lack of spiritual care. Teachers began to focus more on academic content, educational presentation and a stronger intellectual environment. Enrollment was neglected, if not forgotten.

Third, the Sunday School was no longer the window of entrée into the local church. More visitors began attending the worship service. In the late '50s, a Southern Baptist report indicated that 69 percent of all new church members in Southern Baptist churches

Authorities have come to recognize that the worship platform attracts visitors to the local church, but they are bonded into the church family through small groups.

came into the church through the Sunday School. In the late 1980s, Southern Baptists reported less than 10 percent of new membership came into the church through Sunday School.

Fourth, the bonding element of enrollment was lost to the church. Authorities have come to recognize that the worship platform attracts visitors to the local church, but they are bonded into the church family through small groups. Because most churches often do not have small groups, the Sunday School has been the bonding instrument over the years. As a result, when Sunday School enrollment was phased out, that bonding element to local churches was lost.

To compensate, churches have had to do the following:

- Emphasize a stronger platform of music, entertainment and/or communication;
- Use cells/Bible studies to provide a bonding element;

- Suffer a loss of church loyalty;
- Experience a loss of doctrinal loyalty;
- Endure a loss in financial loyalty.

Enrollment Important to Sunday School

The following suggestions are offered on how to turn your Sunday School around:

1. A Sunday School should target those people who only attend worship. Because most visitors attend the worship service, the Sunday School should fish in this pond for prospects.

    How can they get a visitor into the Sunday School? Not by offering the advantages of study or an educational environment. Most people are not interested in additional education. What visitors need is fellowship and involvement. Therefore, people who attend worship should be invited to attend adult Bible fellowship.

2. A Sunday School should create an administered program to systematically incorporate prospects into the Sunday School. This is a strategy of enrolling friends and neighbors into Bible study. Create a new window of entrée into the local body through Sunday School enrollment.

3. Begin using the term "Bible study" rather than Sunday School. While Sunday School may be a barrier to many adults, the term "Bible study" describes what you do. People are interested in Bible study with fellowship. This places a primary focus on fellowship with others who are pursuing answers in God's Word.

4. Target adults. Many people think of Sunday School as a children's organization, but adults comprise 51 percent of the Sunday School population.

> ## SUNDAY SCHOOL ATTENDANCE
> ## BY PERCENTAGE
>
> **Adults**   **51 percent**
> **Youth**   **12 percent**
> **Children**   **37 percent**

5. Move away from communicating only by lectures, speeches and talks. Make Sunday School an exciting fellowship where adults get to know one another, care for one another and study the Bible together.

6. Change the title of teacher to leader. Call them leaders because they are Bible study leaders, spiritual life leaders, outreach leaders and prayer leaders. This title moves the focus from talking, speeches and someone up front lecturing. Although they will continue to teach God's Word, a change in title will change people's perception (i.e., their perception of what the class leader does and the expectation of what they will get from the class).

   The role of the Bible study leader must change to provide spiritual care to everyone in the class. The leader must follow up on absentees, help people solve their problems and bond people into adult Bible fellowships.

7. Helping students take responsibility for their class is another way to turn around your Sunday School. By focusing on enrollment, students realize it is their duty to bond prospects into the class. When they recognize their responsibility to the whole class, they will check on missing class members and will offer spiritual help to their friends.

8. Change the name from Sunday School to adult Bible

fellowship. The focus is no longer on education or an academic environment. Focus on fellowship. Call the class an adult Bible fellowship because fellowship by itself is not enough. It should be fellowship based on the Word of God.

Three Types of Contacts

Three kinds of contacts or visits can be made for a Sunday School: (1) soul-winning contacts; (2) contacting absentees to get them back; and (3) contacting prospects to enroll them in Bible study.

Class outreach should center on the priority that will produce the greatest results. Approximately 80 percent of the outreach contacts should be to absentees because the class has an obligation to them and they are the easiest group to get back into the class.

Fifteen percent of the outreach contacts are with prospects, attempting to enroll them in Bible study. This is the second easiest group to get into the class. Approximately 5 percent of the contacts will be to win souls for Christ. Although this is the most important thing a church does, it is not always the easiest to accomplish.

Some people are reluctant to go on soul-winning visitations. They have never won a soul for Christ and it may scare them. Usually they make any excuse to avoid such a visit. Use those people in absentee follow-up because they are most likely to get results with absentees. Also, they are contacting someone they know, so no barriers are present.

Many people will make an enrollment contact because it does not carry the life-or-death obligation of soul winning. It is easy to ask someone if he/she is interested in enrolling in Bible study. Even then, if someone says no, that rejection is easier to accept.

Because workers are talking about their class, they won't feel that they have been rebuked, nor has the person rejected the gospel. The person simply has not chosen to enroll in Bible study. A polite response by the workers will make it possible for that prospect to be invited at a later time. Also, a polite response may lead to a conversation about Bible study.

How to Enroll a Person in Bible Study

When attempting to get people through the Sunday School window of entrée into Bible study ask, "Are you interested in enrolling in Bible study?" This gives an opportunity to explain what they will experience in an adult Bible fellowship.

First, explain that it is a Bible fellowship, not a class. Explain that you have coffee and time to visit, you do not just sit in chairs and listen to lectures. Then explain how people ask questions and talk to one another.

A visit to enroll someone in Bible study can be called a "chocolate chip cookie visit." Because friends share their homemade baking with their friends, take homemade cookies to prospects with a view of being friendly.

This is a completely different strategy from taking your Bible with a view of leading them to Christ. Your cookies let them know you love them. When the conversation is ripe ask, "Are you interested in Bible study?" Point out that friends attend adult Bible fellowship where they have fun, interact and have an opportunity to apply God's Word to their lives.

TWENTY-FOUR PLACES TO ENROLL PEOPLE IN BIBLE STUDY*

1. When people "join the church," they are enrolled in the Sunday School.

2. Enroll church members who are not enrolled in Sunday School.
3. Enroll visitors in the church service.
4. Enroll relatives.
5. Enroll newly married couples in the church or community.
6. Enroll couples expecting children.
7. Enroll people who move into the neighborhood.
8. Enroll through a phone survey.
9. Enroll people who have signed the church guest book.
10. Enroll people by placing enrollment cards in the church pews or racks.
11. Clip an enrollment card to each prospect card sent out on visitation.
12. Go door-to-door in specific areas around the church to enroll people in Bible study.
13. At special music programs, vacation Bible study programs, Christmas programs, etc. clip enrollment cards to the programs and ask visitors to enroll.
14. Ask the pastor to include an enrollment card with each letter he sends to visitors.
15. Conduct parents enrollment campaign after VBS.
16. Conduct a mail campaign to enroll people in Bible study.
17. Stand at back of auditorium and enroll visitors to the church or those who should be in Bible study.
18. Give visitors to Sunday School an enrollment card instead of a visitor's card. If they know they can't return, have them scratch out *enrollment* and write in *visitor.*
19. Conduct a direct mail campaign to parents of children who come to Sunday School.
20. Have people who fill out visitor slips in church write "enroll me" across the top.

21. Make a "cookie visit" and ask people to enroll in Bible study.

22. Conduct a "yes-seeker" campaign among class members, asking everyone to seek out five people, asking them to enroll in Bible study.

23. Conduct a "sign-up" campaign among class members and recognize the member who enrolls the largest number of people for Bible study.

24. Recognize everyone who was a "yes-seeker" and invite them to share their experiences in inviting people to enroll in Bible study.

*Taken from *Sunday School Enrollment*, a resource packet for church leaders to teach to workers to prepare them for using Sunday School enrollment techniques. Published by Church Growth Institute, P.O. Box 4404, Lynchburg, VA 24502.

5
Everything Starts
with Sunday School

Second Baptist Church
Houston, Texas

Dr. Edwin Young, Pastor

ONE OF THE LARGEST AND MOST STRATEGIC CHURCHES IN AMERICA also has one of the most unique adult Sunday School programs because it does not confine itself to the format suggested by its denominational educators.

"We do all our ministry through the Sunday School," said Dr. Edwin Young, pastor of the Second Baptist Church in Houston, Texas, and president of the 15-million-member Southern Baptist Convention. This is a strong statement considering that many churches are giving up on Sunday School.

Each week the Houston church averages more than 12,000 in worship services and 9,000 in Sunday School. Each year it receives an income of approximately $20 million and baptizes more than 1,000 converts.

Some people believe the $34-million worship center, which was built in 1985 and seats 6,200, is the most beautiful worship center of its size in the country. The 5-story-tall stained glass windows are breathtaking.

Helping People Build a Church

Each adult class is coeducational, having a man and woman alternating every other week as the teacher. The smallest adult class has 30 members, the largest 300. Each class has a director who is responsible for effectively running each class and 9 other people under his/her direction to coordinate various areas, including class ministry, missions and recreation.

Despite the church's size, it is difficult to hide there. Visitors to the church will be contacted. A dropout will be invited to play basketball, to sing in the choir, to join a prayer team, to work in the nursery, to become involved in a small shepherd group or to attend a church outreach party.

In 1979, when Young became the pastor, approximately 300

people attended the Sunday School. Today, more than 20 times that number are present.

Sunday School Didn't Just Happen

"Our Sunday School structure did not come into place suddenly," Young explained. "It grew out of a passion to reach people. We didn't sit down and draw this on a chart; it grew out of helping people and building a church."

When Young arrived, he began several other programs, using the same people as leaders. First, he beefed up the Training Union on Sunday evening and inaugurated a strong mission outreach. Later, those same leaders were recruited to work in small groups, following Ralph Neighbor's small-group concept. The result was counterproductive.

"We were wiping out our leaders," Young said, "because we were using them seven days a week."

Today, he said, "We do everything through the Sunday School." All other programs flow through it or rise to support it.

Sunday School Fuels the Church

As a result, the church runs its small groups, discipleship training, fellowship and sports program through the Sunday School. The majority of adult Bible study classes meet in the Family Life Building, a massive brick building surrounded by a parking lot as large as a modern-day shopping mall.

When entering the building, the visitor is confronted by a three-story atrium that has a mirrored wall reaching from the first to the top floor. Water splashes in a fountain; the floors sparkle with marble, and touches of elegance are present everywhere.

On a Sunday morning, a visitor may see 40 carts with coffee

containers, each waiting to be rolled down the hall for use in an adult Bible study class. The class supplies the doughnuts, but the church supplies the coffee because it believes in Bible study with fellowship.

The church has three gymnasiums—the original gym and a new, modern Olympic-size facility that divides into two sections. Because of the modern weight room, lockers and positive surroundings, members of the Houston Rockets basketball team work out there most weeks.

When asked the secret of growth, Young responds, "Leadership, leadership, leadership."

. . . .

The Secret Word to Growth
When asked the secret of growth, Young responds, "Leadership, leadership, leadership."

He believes that pastors lead from their knees, where they get their vision from God, and that the visionary pastor is the key to leadership.

Worship also contributed to the church's growth, Young said. "We work on worship, looking at worship as the bride—beautiful for Christ." Young stated that a pastor must plan, prepare, evaluate, then be ready to change to improve worship each week.

The adult Sunday School is another source of growth. The Houston church reported that 85 percent of its Sunday School is adult.

Do Not Call It Sunday School

"We don't call it Sunday School," Young said. "Adults think Sunday School is only for children." So the church calls it Bible study.

Young explained that many visitors are from denominations other than Southern Baptist who believe that Sunday School is for children. "We do not want to use that barrier term; rather we want to use a function—what they are doing, rather than a description—what they are."

Two Teachers to a Class

Every adult class has two teachers, a man and woman, but they are never husband and wife. Thirty-five minutes are devoted to teaching the Word of God during each class.

Because they teach every other Sunday, teachers have 14 days to prepare. Young estimated that the average adult teacher in his church devoted about 24 hours to preparation for each lesson.

"The secret of the successful class is the giftedness of leadership," the pastor noted. "I'll take a risk and use a new Christian who has the gift of teaching in that task rather than put an old Christian there without that gift."

Young believes that many Sunday Schools fail because they use fine, wonderful Christians who don't have the gift of teaching.

Director Must Make Class Go, Grow

A director who manages each class must have the gift of administration or leadership. This is a lay person who is expected to make the class go and grow, not the teacher.

Most of the people who are coordinators in the adult Sunday

School class have the gift of shepherding. So adults in Bible study follow those who have the gift of group leadership and those who have the gift of teaching feed the class.

When Young observed the great Bible-teaching churches in the north, he noted their deep commitment to communicate the Word of God. But when he examined the classes deeply, he failed to find outreach or growth.

When Young examined the great Southern Baptist churches, he found outreach but not a depth of Bible teaching and individual growth in the Word of God. He believes adult classes at the Second Baptist Church in Houston represent a balance of good Bible teaching and aggressive outreach.

Young believes the key to the success of his church's Sunday School is the presence of two gifted persons. The first has a passion to teach the Word of God. The second person is a Sunday School class director who has the gift of administration and is successful in involving everyone in the class to work.

Director and Nine Coordinators Lead Classes

Working under a director, each Sunday School class has nine coordinators or workers, each with a separate task that makes the class function.

1. Shepherd group coordinator—The main purpose of this leader is "inreach." He or she places people in shepherd groups that usually meet once a month for fellowship, discussion and to build relationships. These groups are not primarily for Bible study. Whereas many churches are organizing a small-group ministry *apart* from Sunday School, Second Baptist Church does it *through* Sunday School. In a true sense, the shepherd group coordinator is really the pastor of the class. This person has a committee of shepherd leaders to help in shepherding responsibility.

2. Outreach coordinator—This person should have the gift of evangelism. The outreach coordinator meets all visitors each Sunday morning. The class secretary is responsible to the outreach coordinator, who works with him or her to provide information about prospects. The outreach coordinator guides the visitation teams who follow up in the homes of all visitors. When names are given to the class from the church, the outreach coordinator makes sure that the prospects are contacted.

3. Discipleship coordinator—This person is responsible for the discipling branch of the class. He or she is responsible for training leaders and developing disciples. The Southern Baptists' *MasterLife* program is taught through the class and is supervised by the discipleship coordinator. In a sense, the traditional Southern Baptist Training Union (BTU), which used to meet every Sunday evening before church, is now organized and administered through the adult Bible class. Some of the discipleship activities meet on Sunday afternoon, and some meet on Monday or Tuesday evenings.

The prayer coordinator works under the discipleship coordinator. Second Baptist Church has an outstanding prayer program. Beginning in 1985, it began a chain of prayer in the prayer chapel that has not been broken since it was inaugurated. Someone is always at the church on his or her knees praying. Those who pray at the church are described as a part of the First Watch.

Others are unable to meet at the church but have committed to pray for one hour each week at home. They are called the Second Watch. More than 1,100 people pray in the Second Watch. (The term comes from Jesus who said, "What, could you not watch with Me one hour?" [Matthew 26:40].) The prayer coordinator makes sure that enough people keep the prayer chain going.

4. The social coordinator—This person plans the outreach events, which bring outsiders into the class. These may be class parties, fellowships or any other events to promote the social life of the church. People with the gift of hospitality are well suited for this job.

5. Nursery coordinator—Second Baptist Church's two-story nursery building has enough rooms for every two months of a baby's growth cycle. The nursery building is larger than most church buildings. Obviously, a vast number of volunteers are needed to operate the nursery. The coordinator not only recruits, but also makes sure that those who sign up actually show up for the job. This person must have the gift of helps or service.

6. Special projects coordinator—This person coordinates volunteers for the large-scale special events that are conducted by Second Baptist Church, such as the Christmas program, revivals, the Electric Light Parade and Angels of Light at Christmas, and other outreach programs.

7. Choir recruiter—The choir recruiter operates under the special projects coordinator and is responsible primarily for recruiting people for the two church choirs. Approximately 450 choir members sing in each of the two morning choirs.

8. Recreation coordinator—The Second Baptist Church sponsors 72 softball teams, stretching from small children and T-ball, up to senior saints doing "slow-pitch" softball. The teams only represent part of the picture. The church also sponsors 280 teams for men and women involved in 45 athletic leagues including basketball, flag football, softball and volleyball.

The recreation coordinator tries to fill approximately one-half to one-third of each team with nonchurched prospects. The recreation coordinator works only with adult teams. The children's teams are coordinated by the athletic department of the church.

The church campus contains five softball fields, a football field, a soccer field and three gymnasiums. Also included are racquetball courts, eight bowling lanes, a weight room and an aerobics room.

9. Ministry network coordinator—The main responsibility of this person is to involve class members in ministry. He or she seeks to involve people in the various support groups of the church, including those for the handicapped, those with addictions, prisoners, crisis pregnancy groups and so on.

Second Baptist does not follow the traditional approach of small, adult classes; the classes are organized to use the best Bible teaching available, to nurture members and to provide an evangelistic outreach.

Church Ministries Revitalized

Second Baptist Church in Houston, Texas, has revitalized its total ministry by involving adults through the various ministries of the Bible study classes. Rather than follow the traditional approach of small, adult classes, the classes are organized to use the best Bible teaching available, to nurture members and to provide an evangelistic outreach. The success of this church argues its approach.

Ministry Application

BIBLE STUDY CLASS STRUCTURE

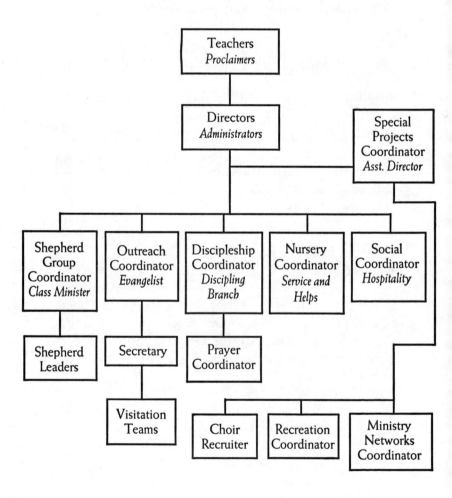

6
Bus Outreach Fuels Growth

First Assembly of God
Phoenix, Arizona

Rev. Tommy Barnett, Pastor

"EVERY MEMBER IS A MINISTER" IS A MOTTO THAT HELPS FUEL THE growth of First Assembly of God church in Phoenix, Arizona. Under the leadership of Tommy Barnett, church attendance has grown from 250 in December 1979, to more than 10,000 today.

The church has constructed a 6,500-seat auditorium, one of the largest church auditoriums in Arizona, located on Shadow Mountain, 20 miles north of the downtown area.

The church sponsors spectacular events such as an Easter passion play that has attracted more than 150,000 people, the "Living Christmas Tree" at Christmas, and the "Living Flag" on the Fourth of July.

Other factors contributing to the growth of First Assembly of God are the evangelistic preaching of Barnett and more than 140 ministries that reach out to the hungry, the addicted and the HIV-positive people in Phoenix.

A Unique Bus Ministry

One of the pillars beneath this massive church is its unique bus ministry.

When Barnett arrived in Phoenix, he started with two buses. He acknowledged that the idea of a bus was a novelty in Phoenix, but he made it work.

Barnett previously pastored West Side Assembly of God church in Davenport, Iowa, which also used buses extensively. He developed a national reputation for building a fast-growing church.

Between 1971 to 1979, the Iowa church grew from an average of 76 attenders each week to 4,400 during his last year there. In 1976, he was recognized for having built the fastest growing Sunday School in the United States. *Christian Life* magazine selected Barnett as "One of the Ten Sunday School Newsmakers of the Decade."

Pastor Sought Challenge in Phoenix

Barnett left Iowa when things were going well. He said he wanted to go to a big city that offered a big challenge. His challenge resulted in a Phoenix congregation of 250 people, who built a $12-million sanctuary during the first 5 years of his ministry there.

"These were probably the most unlikely church members to ever construct a building like this," Barnett said. "They were not wealthy and not outstanding in the community; they were just a group of people who loved to win souls.

"The building is just a tool. We use the church to build people rather than using the people to build the church."

Barnett loves to break records. Within three weeks of arriving in December 1979, he held a Christmas rally that attracted 2,700 people to a single event. Within a year, attendance exploded to more than 4,800 at an Easter rally and more than 8,000 at a Christmas rally a year later.

The church grew so rapidly that in October 1981 *Moody* magazine and the International Christian Education Association recognized him as having built the "Fastest Growing Church in America." The following year the church again was honored when the average weekly attendance reached 5,462.

Church Used Public Facilities

To accommodate Sunday School growth, the church leased the facilities of two city schools and a number of classes were held around picnic tables in city parks and in other public arenas.

Anyone can draw a crowd, but the strength of Barnett is in his preaching the gospel and giving an altar call. As many as 1,600 people have responded to such calls. Even though he is an Assembly of God preacher, Barnett has said on several occasions that he learned to give an altar call from his father, and was inspired to build a great church by Baptist churches. "But, I get power from the pentecostal experience," he said.

Dream Big

Barnett is an outstanding leader because he dreams big. When he came to the Phoenix church of 250 people, he began to lift their vision.

The local newspaper noted, "When Barnett, 47, handsome and perpetually hoarse from preaching, hit town from Iowa 5 years ago, he took over the 250-member Phoenix First Assembly of God in downtown Phoenix. He made the congregation see a huge new church filled with 5,000 people every week."

From the very beginning, he stretched the congregation's faith to see a church on Shadow Mountain, to see thousands coming to receive Christ, to see the power of God.

Barnett's dream for the Phoenix church was a bus ministry, which he says "is still the greatest way to reach souls for Christ!"

··

Busing Is Greatest Way to Reach Souls

Part of Barnett's dream for the Phoenix church was a bus ministry, which he says "is still the greatest way to reach souls for Christ!"

For many years, buses were used only to reach children, but the dream was expanded to include adults. Today, the church dispatches 36 buses throughout south Phoenix on Sunday afternoon to pick up children and their parents. They transport them 20 miles to the north Phoenix church where they are fed a Sunday night meal, attend the Sunday night service and many are led to Jesus Christ.

Blitzing a Block an Hour

"We just blitz a block in one hour," Barnett said in describing a Sunday afternoon work period. "Our workers go to every home on a block inviting everyone to church.

"We go to a place and get as many parents and children as we can to ride a bus to our facility on the north side." He explained that children cannot come on Sunday night if their parents do not attend.

Saturday Morning Sunday School

The bus ministry begins on Saturday morning when workers visit the south side of Phoenix. A different group uses the same buses on Saturday afternoon to reach different children for a second Sunday School in different locations.

The Saturday bus ministry takes children to a prearranged place on the south side for Bible teaching, which can take place in an indoor school, an outdoor picnic table or any other place they have determined that a crowd can gather.

Sometimes a stage is set up to present the gospel by the outdoor children's church. The program is repeated on Saturday afternoon.

A Twelve-mile Sunday Outreach

On Sunday morning, the buses run in the immediate middle-class neighborhood surrounding Shadow Mountain, bringing children to the main church location. Approximately 1,500 are brought to the church for Sunday School every Sunday morning.

The Sunday morning routes around the main church reach out in a 12-mile radius. The children are bused to the gymnasium for Sunday School and children's church.

Because of the nature of the community, the children who travel on Sunday morning to the main location have difficulty getting their parents to ride a bus with them on Sunday night, so those routes are not run again on Sunday. The south-side children are brought to the church on Sunday night.

"We feel those children who ride the bus on Sunday morning can get their parents to drive them to the Sunday evening service," Barnett said.

An inner-city church is located on the south side of Phoenix and seven houses in that area are used for ministry. This is more of a mission outreach. This ministry to the poor and minorities includes feeding, clothing and helping meet temporal needs.

Workers Make the Program Work

To run such a vast program requires a great number of dedicated workers who will go out two or three times a weekend to make the program happen.

Young People Committed to Work

"One of the greatest things that has helped us carry out our mission is the Master's Commission," Barnett explained.

The Master's Commission involves 75 young people who commit one year to the Lord's work. Those young people come from all over the United States to be trained for Christian service.

Barnett described this program as similar to the Mormons

who spend time as missionaries before entering their vocation or profession. More than half of those in the Master's Commission come from other churches, many of them Assembly of God churches.

The young people live in the homes of Phoenix church members, who provide room and board for one year. The young people come to the church and pray from 7:00 to 8:00 each morning. From 8:00 A.M. to 9:00 A.M. they memorize Scripture and from 9:00 A.M. to 11:00 A.M. they study the Berean Bible course, which is similar to a Bible institute course and which leads to various levels of ordination.

"In 1991, the young people from the Master's Commission led over 100,000 people to the Lord," Barnett noted. "About half of our bus routes are operated by the Master's Commission."

If people believe in what you're doing and believe in God's dream, they'll jump in and break their necks and just do it. Barnett wanted to go to a big city because there are no limits to what can happen there because there are no limits with God.

Deacons, Deaconesses Follow Up

More than 300 deacons and deaconesses conduct visitations and follow-ups. The city is separated by zip codes, and deacons and deaconesses follow up on any visitor to the church as well as visit and care for existing church families. They are asked to visit two hours each week and are given cards, which they use to follow up on church visitors.

Barnett indicated that he plans to continue constructing Sunday School buildings. The church offers 36 adult elective classes, some of which prepare people for ministry. A few are permanent classes based on fellowship and cohesiveness, one class is devoted to soul winning and other classes cover books of the Bible.

Many of the classes meet in the church auditorium because of a classroom shortage. The largest class consists of 250 people. More than 10,000 people are involved in the Saturday School, the Sunday School and the outreach ministries of the church.

I Believe in People

"I believe in people," Barnett said. "I know a lot of pastors who say that people won't work, but if people believe in what you are doing and believe in God's dream, they'll do it. They'll jump in and break their necks and they'll just do it.

"When I decided I wanted to be in a big city," Barnett said, "I knew that there are no limits to what can happen here because there are no limits with God."

Ministry Application

The Bus Captain

1. The success or failure of a bus route depends on the spiritual commitment of the bus captain.
2. The bus captain must take ownership for the ministry in his or her assigned area.
3. The bus captain is to attempt to fill his or her bus with

people every week. This requires approximately three hours of visitation a week.

4. The bus captain must have a heart for children because most of the riders will be children.
5. This position falls under the general responsibility of the bus director.
6. The bus captain will attend the public services of our church, including Sunday School, morning and evening services and mid-week services. "Moreover, it is required in stewards [bus captains] that one be found faithful" (1 Cor. 4:2).
7. All bus workers are asked to attend the teachers' and officers' meeting each week.
8. Bus captains are responsible to see that their team is informed of the procedures and rules of the bus program of our church. Should a problem develop, the captain should attempt to deal with it while it is small and can be handled easily and quickly.
9. The bus captain should visit the houses and people in the area assigned to him or her.

   a. In establishing or maintaining a route, it is necessary to go door-to-door, combing the area for people who do not attend church.
   b. Leave a brochure at each new house.
   c. After the route is established and a person rides the bus, revisit that person every Saturday and recommit that person for the following Sunday.
   d. The object of the visit is to commit people to ride the bus on Sunday. Of course, if the opportunity presents itself, try to meet any need you may discover. Remember, Saturday visitation is to commit riders for the next day.

10. Use your assistant captain, workers, secretary, etc. to assist you in visitations. This not only multiplies your efforts, but also provides an opportunity for them to learn how to build and to maintain a route.

7
Sunday Evening Sunday School

Grove City Church of the Nazarene
Grove City, Ohio

Rev. Bob Huffaker, Pastor

THE GROVE CITY CHURCH OF THE NAZARENE, LOCATED A FEW miles south of the Columbus, Ohio, belt line, faced some real challenges late in 1990. Attendance had increased to the point that a second morning worship service was needed, and Pastor Bob Huffaker believed that sandwiching a Sunday School between the two services would pose a problem.

"What I had read about flip-flopping Sunday School and worship services would have produced hassle," he said.

No Need for Evening Preaching Service
Huffaker also believed the congregation did not need another preaching service on Sunday evening. He recognized that he, like most pastors, put most of his emphasis on preparing for Sunday morning because that is when the crowd attended, including visitors and casual attendees.

Although he loved preaching Sunday evening, he did not have the same depth of commitment to his Sunday evening sermon as he did to the Sunday morning sermon.

To further complicate the dilemma, the Sunday evening service had been focused on an evangelistic outreach. In previous years, the Grove City Church of the Nazarene, as most American churches, had visitors come on Sunday evening. That had been the time to preach the gospel, to conduct an evangelistic song service and to lead the lost to Christ.

Huffaker recognized, however, that visitors rarely attended on Sunday night anymore, including many of his Sunday morning visitors. Sunday night was no longer an effective evangelistic outreach.

It was more logical, Huffaker concluded, to focus his Sunday evening hour on education and his Sunday morning service on worship.

Focus on Evening Sunday School

It is not easy to sell a church on Sunday evening Sunday School, especially if people had never done it that way before. When Huffaker first mentioned the change to his church, some members were opposed even though he explained that such a plan had worked while he pastored in Hereford, Texas.

Meanwhile, changes were being made in the traditional Nazarene Sunday morning service and many baby boomers from the Grove City suburbs were beginning to attend the church.

Pastor Asked the People

Huffaker wanted to have an alive "praise and worship celebration" type of service that would appeal to young couples. When he tried that, the length of the traditional one-hour worship was curtailed.

Huffaker developed three options that included the positive and negative features of each proposal. The options were first shown to the church board, the Sunday School teachers and to other people in leadership. (See Ministry Application)

The church was asked to make a six-month commitment to the evening Sunday School. It usually is easier to persuade people to try a new thing if you call it an "experiment." Huffaker promised that after six months the church would review the results of Sunday evening Sunday School and would proceed from there.

Reluctance to Change

A few adults did not want to make the change; therefore, one adult Sunday morning class was offered for those who could not or would not attend in the evening. That Sunday School class meets at 9:15 A.M. for an hour and about 20 members in this class attend the second worship service. This was an important concession to those who otherwise might have opposed the entire project.

The church did not offer any Sunday School for children in the morning. The boomers wanted their children in children's church while they were in the main sanctuary. So the Grove City Church of the Nazarene offered church for children while the boomers were worshiping. On Sunday morning the family

A church should not change to a Sunday evening Sunday School just for the numbers but also for quality.

came together, worshiped together and left together. It was only logical that without adult classes, the church could not offer children's classes.

After they decided to go to the Sunday evening Sunday School, some people complained about not having Sunday evening preaching or what many called the Sunday night evangelistic service.

Addressing this problem, Huffaker decided to use the month with five Sundays to have a large evangelistic rally. This meant that every quarter the church had an old-fashioned, Sunday night revival meeting. This addition seemed to satisfy those who were saying the church was getting away from Sunday evening preaching.

A church should not change to a Sunday evening Sunday School just for the numbers but also for quality, Huffaker said. While describing how quality was improved, he observed, "People are not as rushed, children haven't been grabbed out of bed without breakfast and people are not running from Sunday School to worship."

On Sunday evening, the pastor leads the entire church in a family worship period from 6:00 to 6:30, which includes singing, special songs, offering and testimonies.

Following the worship period, the people attend Sunday School classes in a relaxed study of the Word without interruption. In such a casual atmosphere, many couples will stay for a time of fellowship and recreation.

Because the pastor is not obligated to preach a message, he is given the opportunity to conduct membership and other specialized classes and occasionally to visit Sunday School classes.

Home Studies Freed Classrooms

Another advantage is that it allows for such options as cell groups and Bible studies in homes while the children meet at the church for Sunday School. This also frees up classrooms at the church.

An advantage to conducting Sunday School during the evening is that there is more room to grow and more parking spaces are available.

Also helpful is the fact that the church does not have to provide two full music programs on Sunday morning: one for worship (both worship services have identical music), the other for Sunday School.

After two years in the program, Huffaker noted that attendance has tripled on Sunday evening, though this does not mean Sunday School attendance has tripled. In September of 1990, average attendance was 491; by September of 1992, the average attendance was up to 590, a gain of 100.

Sunday Evening Advantages

Huffaker said the first advantage to conducting Sunday School during the evening is that there is more room to grow and more parking spaces are available. The parking lot empties during the 30-minute break between the 2 Sunday morning services and provides parking space for the second service.

Sunday evening Sunday School provides time for leaders to diversify their classes and to use films and videos, the pastor noted.

Evening Attire More Casual

Another advantage is that "people can dress casual," Huffaker said. "This is a plus because it removes one barrier that keeps some from coming.

"On Sunday morning, we were time-bound and people were rushing from Sunday School to church. With 30 minutes between worship services, people have more time to fellowship with one another, which added another plus to our church. Also, the choir has a 30-minute break between the first and second service as does the orchestra."

Huffaker believes an identical type of worship was needed in both services. "I didn't want people to have to make a selection in the type of worship they wanted to attend." In an age when some churches are offering two different types of worship services, this church has chosen to make them identical.

When it comes to preparing sermons, Huffaker pointed out

that his focus during the week is on the high point, the sermon he will deliver on Sunday morning. Therefore, his personal prayer time, message, preparation and focus is more pointed. Under the new schedule, he does not have to prepare two sermons but preaches one sermon twice. "I love it," he said.

Board Unanimous in Its Support

A year after moving Sunday School to the evening, the board members reviewed the change and were unanimous about continuing, noting it had been a positive move for the church.

By moving Sunday School to the evening, the Church of the Nazarene in Grove City, Ohio, was able to introduce two innovative Sunday morning services and to triple the Sunday evening Sunday School attendance.

Ministry Application

Sunday Evening Class Sizes

A variety of sizes of adult classes are offered on Sunday evening at the Grove City Church of the Nazarene. Some are large classes ranging from 50 to 100. Other classes have only 5 or 10 in attendance; most classes average 20.

Types of Subject Matter Taught

1. A "Just Grads" class meets the needs of those who have recently graduated from high school.
2. A young singles class is offered for those in their mid- to upper-20s and who are not yet married.
3. Several classes have members ranging in age from 25 to 60. Classes are not organized by age and certainly are not

mandated by that criteria. People can attend wherever they wish and they have the opportunity to change classes, according to variable subjects.

4. One class operates primarily on a discussion-question/ answer basis, another by the Nazarene quarterly calendar and another by 80 percent lecture and 20 percent audio/ video assistance. The latter class is designed primarily for those interested in in-depth research and study, focusing on topical studies.

5. A senior-citizen class is offered during the first morning worship service so that seniors can attend the second worship service. Most of those people have difficulty getting out at night and this class meets their needs. Meeting people's needs is the key to a successful Sunday School program.

Sunday Evening Attire

Approximately 90 percent of the men in the morning worship services wear suits or sports coats with ties, and approximately 98 percent of the women wear dresses. In the evening Sunday School period, approximately 25 percent of the men wear suits or sports coats with ties, and nearly 75 percent wear dress shirts without a tie, or a pullover sweater. Nearly 25 percent of the men wear jeans. Sunday evening, approximately 40 percent of the women wear slacks or jeans. This figure varies, according to the weather and season.

Sunday Evening Curriculum

Only three adult classes use the Nazarene Sunday School curriculum. The Bible-studies class uses only the Bible as its primary source. One class encourages its members to purchase a popular Christian book and to study its contents.

One class uses TLC (Tender Loving Care), written by Dale Galloway of the New Life Community Church in Portland, Oregon. This is the curriculum used by small groups that meet during the week in homes for outreach, fellowship and pastoral care. A couple of classes vary considerably in their studies—from videos by James Dobson or Tim LaHaye to audios by Chuck Swindoll or Charles Stanley.

Conclusion

Growth was slow at first in Sunday evening Sunday School, but has increased. The church has been pleased with the results. The quality of classes has improved, people have relaxed and staff and congregation have felt less pressure.

OPTION I
(SANDWICH)

1st Service	8:30 - 9:30 A.M.
Sunday School	9:45 - 10:30 A.M.
2nd Service	10:40 - 12:00 Noon

POSITIVES
1. Least amount of change
2. Could provide two worship styles
3. We have done it before
4. For Sunday School—can still use classrooms adjoining sanctuary
5. Accommodates visitors
6. This change makes for least amount of confusion

NEGATIVES
1. Transporting youth to other buildings
2. Less Sunday School time and space
3. Demands more of choir members' time
4. Greater work load and pressure on staff and choir
5. Choir in one service only, could not function as class teachers, as well as class members
6. Less time for worship
7. Does not relieve parking pressures

OPTION II
(FLIP-FLOP)

1st Service	8:30 - 10:00 A.M.
2nd Service	10:30 - 12:00 Noon
Sunday School	9:15 - 10:15 A.M.

POSITIVES

1. More space
2. Shorter time required for staff and choir
3. Provides more room for Sunday School
4. Later worship
5. Choir in both services

NEGATIVES

1. Force adults to use children's classrooms
2. Administrative hassles
3. Two separate churches
4. Congested parking
5. Mandates which service you attend
6. Could not use Sunday School room opening into sanctuary
7. Eliminates freedom of choice for Sunday School classes
8. Time goes past 12:00 noon

OPTION III
(SUNDAY-NIGHT SPECIAL)

1st Service	9:00 - 10:30 A.M.
Sunday School	9:30 - 10:30 A.M.
Sunday School	10:45 - 11:45 A.M.
Worship	6:00 - 6:30 P.M.
Sunday School	6:30 - 7:30 P.M.

POSITIVES
1. Flexibility
2. More room for growth
3. More evangelistic Sunday School
4. More parking
5. More diversified Sunday School
6. Time frame is flexible
7. Great time for fellowship after class
8. Good time for prayer groups to meet
9. Double the evening service attendance
10. Less stress and pressure on staff and choir
11. Focus on morning worship
12. Focus on evening Sunday School
13. Opportunity for Pastor's Class
14. Sunday School in morning option
15. Not rushed for Sunday School
16. Two full music programs

NEGATIVES
1. Transportation with older adults
2. Major change
3. First-timers wouldn't come back Sunday night
4. No evangelistic evening service
5. It is not a statistic builder

8

Sunday Schools That Multiply

Skyline Wesleyan Church
Lemon Grove, California

Dr. John Maxwell, Pastor

Skyline Wesleyan Church has one of the most innovative Sunday Schools in America because of: (1) the equipping role of the teachers; (2) the growth through multiple Sunday Schools; and (3) the leadership of Dr. John Maxwell, senior pastor, who understands how to manage change for church growth.

When teachers are asked what their main contribution is to their class, they do not answer, "My communication of content, my Bible knowledge or my teaching skills."

"I give leadership and vision to the class," responded a teacher. By this, the teachers realize their main task is to give direction to the class.

"We are an equipping church," said John Maxwell, pastor. He does not see Skyline Wesleyan Church as primarily a praise and worship church like Jack Hayford's church, The Church On The Way, or a Bible-expositional church like John MacArthur's church, Grace Community, or a soul-winning, evangelistic church like Tommy Barnett's. Although Maxwell ministers in these areas, he sees his church's main task as equipping members for ministry. Maxwell sees his main contribution as "a leader of leaders."

Each Sunday School teacher is a class leader, by which they are outreach leaders, spiritual-life leaders, prayer leaders and discipling leaders.

"The main duty of the Sunday School teacher is to equip everyone in the class to become a leader in the church. Every person should minister according to the gifts God has given to him or her," noted Dan Reiland, former minister of education, who is now executive pastor.

Committed to Church Growth

Two morning-worship services and one Sunday School drew 800 to 1,000 people when John Maxwell became the pastor in 1981.

Today, Skyline Wesleyan has 3 Sunday Schools for all ages at its Lemon Grove site and a fourth at a second campus 14 miles away in East County, San Diego, where the church plans to relocate in the mid-'90s.

The church is building a $22-million complex on 110 acres that stretches for one mile along a San Diego freeway. The new location will enable the church to seat 5,000 people for worship.

"We were committed to church growth, but we were facility-bound," said Dan Reiland, who led the move to two Sunday Schools during the 1980s. "That is where our visitors first attended. They came to the sanctuary. Both of the services were filled and we could not grow."

Sunday School is so integral to all that we are, we cannot have a worship service without adding a Sunday School.

Commitment Critical to Growth

Growth, however, is dependent upon a congregational commitment to the Great Commission and not upon the addition of Sunday Schools, said John Maxwell, who is now the senior pastor.

"We plan to go to five Sunday Schools within a year," he added. "The fifth will probably be a Saturday night worship service and a fully graded Sunday School."

"We do not have the space on Sunday morning, so it appears that the next best time is Saturday evening," Reiland said.

"The church must begin a fifth Sunday School and worship service to raise the financial base of the congregation to more than 4,000 to sustain the immediate financial impact of the new property and building," Reiland explained.

"For us, Sunday School is so integral to all that we are, we cannot have a worship service without adding a Sunday School," Reiland added.

Multiple Options Sought

Reiland said that Skyline's goal is to provide as many worship and teaching options as it can. The more options people have in Sunday School, the more they can vary their daily patterns of life. By offering multiple Sunday Schools, people have more choices.

For example, if a family attends the middle-hour worship service, it can attend Sunday School during the first or third hour. Many people who must work at 11:00 A.M. or noon will attend the first Sunday School and the middle worship service.

Another advantage of multiple Sunday Schools is the flexibility to plan worship. Reiland has added Sunday School classes at the first and third hours because everyone wants to attend church at the 9:40 A.M. middle service.

After a class is established at the first or third hour and people are bonded to that class, Reiland may move the class to the middle hour, forcing the people to attend church at the first or third hour. Because attendance at the first and third hours is smaller, this adjustment frees up space in the middle hour for more visitors.

Growth Creates Added Problems

Each time Skyline has added another Sunday School, it has experienced growth. But added attendance did not come without added problems.

"Our primary problems are all based on time issues," Reiland noted, "and these problems spin off the area of parking. If the preacher goes overtime, there is a major people-bottleneck regarding parking, changing classes and moving people into their next location." So three smoothly run Sunday Schools depend upon starting and finishing every hour exactly on time, which rarely happens.

Schedules Always Tight

The church plans on 20 minutes between sessions. Reiland estimated that it requires about 8 minutes to empty and fill a classroom if everything runs on schedule. The younger the age, the greater the difficulty in having a classroom available on time, he added. And it takes longer for infants and toddlers to check in than adults who simply walk into the room and begin drinking coffee and fellowshiping.

Finding teachers is obviously a problem. Reiland mentioned that when multiple sections are offered, only a certain amount of "best" people volunteer to teach. He finds that a person can stay for two hours and serve, but it is unreasonable to ask that person to stay for three hours or to drive between the campuses and teach at both sites. Multiple services doubles, triples and quadruples the number of staff needed to fill all the teaching slots.

The least attended hour is the third hour on Sunday morning. When the church began multiple sections, however, the early hour was the weakest. After a period of time, people gravitated to the early hour and after six years, it is the most popular hour for Sunday School. The middle remains the most popular hour for worship.

Young Adults Meet During Middle Hour

When Reiland began adding Sunday Schools, he put young adults into the middle hour only. Because they tend to be a homogeneous unit, desiring to attend with their friends, they resist being broken up into two groups. Also, that pushes young adults into the early or late church service—the lesser-attended services. For the same reason, this pattern is followed for high schoolers. They want to stay together for fellowship.

Although the Sunday School is for infants through adults during all three sessions, children's church is grouped only for the middle hour.

Children are grouped from first through third grades and fourth through sixth grades. At the fourth service in East County, the church has children's church for only five divisions: nursery, two- and three-year-olds, four- and five-year-olds, first through third grades, and fourth through sixth grades. At the present time, the ministry is dictated by facilities. Only a few rooms are available for Sunday School at East County.

East County Outreach

The attendance growth at the East County site has jumped to approximately 700. However, at the beginning that attendance only represented a crowd who came to watch a performance or to hear the preaching. Maxwell began to preach commitment to the new people, urging them to become involved in membership, stewardship/tithing and service. The crowd filtered down to 500, which still was a significant attendance for most churches in America.

Reiland said a class is successful when attendance reaches approximately 50 or more and people bond into fellowship and become involved in ministry. Then the class is moved into the middle hour. That pushes class members to attend the first or third worship hour.

"We have a simple 'rule of the largest,'" he said, "which means that whoever has the largest class gets the largest rooms and these rooms are available the first and third hour."

Curriculum Choices

The children's curriculum is chosen for the teachers and assigned to them. However, teachers of adults are given a great deal of freedom. Reiland said, "We believe in matching their authority and responsibility to their accountability." As the teachers demonstrate maturity, "we give them equal authority to choose their curriculum, but we do have guidelines to monitor their choices."

Reiland maintains a system of accountability by approving all curriculum choices. "We require text, title and theme for 6 to 12 weeks in advance from each teacher so we have an idea of where they are going with content. When they use printed textbooks or curriculum, we simply take a look at it for approval."

Reiland pointed out that the church is not a curriculum-based, elective-based or content-based Sunday School but a fel-

The worship service is Skyline's reaching arm for Christ; the Sunday School is the teaching, fellowshiping, equipping arm.

lowship-based Sunday School. For example, a young-married class can literally grow through life and then die together. The church groups people so they are not promoted out of the class at any age break. They simply stay together as a group.

Reiland also noted that this bonding helps eliminate people drifting from one hour to another, especially from the first to third hour.

The Purpose of Sunday Schools

The worship service is Skyline's reaching arm for Christ; the Sunday School is the teaching, fellowshiping, equipping arm, Reiland said.

As a result, leadership, shepherding and teaching are qualities required of every adult-class teacher, he said.

People Trained for Ministry

Reiland explained that the teacher exercises his or her leadership by spotting, recruiting and developing people so they can participate in ministry somewhere in the church. The shepherding care of the class is exercised in counseling, social activities and old-fashioned fellowship.

Another value a teacher brings to a class, and by no means less important, is strong Sunday School teaching. "You cannot build a class on poor teaching," Reiland said, "but good teaching alone does not build a class.

"Our people won't tolerate poor teaching. So to work in our Sunday School, a person had better be a good teacher."

The first quality Reiland looks for in recruitment is not in teaching alone. The candidate must first be a good leader and a good shepherd. Then Reiland recruits a person because he or she is an above-average teacher.

Superintendent Serves as Problem-solver

One Sunday School superintendent oversees all of Skyline's schools. This lay person is an elected member of the church board. This person is a troubleshooter, coordinator and problem-solver. The recruitment, training, assigning and empowering of teachers is handled by the minister of education.

The superintendent is the liaison to the local administrative board and serves primarily as an encourager and as a public relations person for the Sunday School staff.

On Sunday mornings, literally dozens of mind-boggling needs and problems arise within a period of four hours at Skyline. The superintendent is responsible to solve these problems as they occur. The superintendent manages the office staff, which is at least a half dozen people each session. The superintendent answers the phone, meets and directs new people to class and helps the ushers when services run overtime.

Results? Growth

What have been the results of adding four Sunday Schools? "Growth," was the immediate response from Maxwell and Reiland.

They said the additional Sunday Schools have facilitated church growth. Every class has outreach people who are looking for visitors in the worship service to bring them to class.

Visitation Unstructured
As such, Skyline does not have a totally structured Sunday School visitation program. Each class follows up visitors and absentees. Names and addresses of visitors to the worship service are given to outreach leaders to contact.

Many of the classes have spotters in the sanctuary who are looking for visitors when they stand to be recognized. Basically, a spotter extends an invitation to attend a class immediately following the worship service.

"It's fun and enthusiastic when four or five spotters go up to one visitor and try to persuade them to attend their class," Reiland said. "This makes visitors really feel wanted."

Friendship Offered

Reiland explained that each class gives different things to entice visitors to a class. For example, one class gave away a mug that changes messages when filled with hot coffee. When hot, it says, "Joint Venture." When cool, it says, "Family Living at Its Best."

Such recruiting practices seldom create problems, Reiland said. "It tends to work because we are so spread out in so many different worship services and not every class is as aggressive as others. I don't think we overdominate or intimidate a guest. Far more guests slip out without an invitation than who get mobbed."

Practical Suggestions

Reiland believes it is not a complicated process to add a second Sunday School if the leadership is committed to church growth. It is not hard to add a second service if the people are committed to soul winning and evangelism and are willing to persevere through what is called "change valley."

Resistance Will Subside

Reiland explained that a "change valley" usually lasts about six months. He noted that many Sunday School leaders in other churches often give up on an additional Sunday School before it has a chance to work.

Because the typical church resists change and will run into things it does not expect, it often gives up. Vision is needed to see beyond the problems to the results of the second service.

"Even though the average church will gain 12 to 15 percent overnight by going to two services," Reiland said, "just adding an additional option is too much effort if people are not committed to the results."

As Skyline added services, it had to move a long-standing

class that had occupied the same room for 25 years and did not want to move. Maxwell and Reiland visited the class to encourage and motivate it, primarily to give the class the big picture of what was happening. Class attendance had decreased and the room was needed for a much larger youth department.

When the class got the big picture, members became excited. One Sunday morning the teacher dressed like Moses and led the people across the four-lane highway to the new classroom in a rented building.

"After six months, they liked the new room so well they would have fought if someone tried to take it away," Reiland said. To him, the problem of persuading the class to move from its established meeting place is the problem in most churches: People just do not like change.

When a church offers more than one Sunday School on Sunday morning, it is going against tradition. The Skyline Wesleyan Church, however, took the risk and offered multiple Sunday Schools on Sunday morning as a part of its strategy for growth.

Ministry Application

Multiplication Principles
1. The Sunday School staff must possess a commitment to growth.
2. The church leadership must be willing to allocate necessary resources.
3. The pastor must support the change from the pulpit.

Strategy for Implementation
1. Communicate the purpose (growth) and goal (add a Sunday

School session) to the church leadership and Sunday School staff first.

2. Communicate the purpose and goal to members of the congregation about two months before the change takes place.

   a. Show them how they will benefit.
   b. Show them how it fits into the big picture.

3. Recruit the additional staff (Sunday School workers) needed before the change. Do not fall into the trap of "double-dipping," using existing volunteers for just a little while. It always will be longer than anticipated, and the risk is high of losing the worker completely. Important principle: think long-term, not short-term.

4. Train the new teachers with your best material. But always keep the vision before them, over their job description or the curriculum. The vision is, of course, the future. Children represent our future.

5. Hang tough through the "change valley." Change meets resistance and creates tension. Expect this for approximately 6 months, (2 months prior and 4 months afterward). However, 80 percent of the opposition will vanish within the first 30 days following the change. Do not give up or give in.

9
Adult Bible Fellowships

The Chapel
Akron, Ohio

Rev. Knute Larson, Pastor

THE CHAPEL, AKRON, OHIO, IS A LARGE CHURCH; THEY HAVE 4,800 in attendance in the 4 morning worship services, and another 1,200 children in the nursery and children's church. The church has 4 morning worship services: 7:45, 9:00, 10:25 and 11:45. In the near future, they plan to restart a Saturday evening "seekers" service. The church receives 4.5 million dollars a year, and like most large churches, it would be difficult for a visitor to crack the "anonymity barrier" because of its size. However, the Adult Bible Fellowships (ABFs) bridge that barrier.

"Visitors to ABFs get the feel of a small church," testifies Knute Larson, pastor since 1983. "When I stand before Christ and He asks me what I have done about the 'one another' commands in the Bible, I will not be embarrassed," said Larson. "I will point to the ABFs, our 'churches within the church.'"

Today, The Chapel has more than 30 Adult Bible Fellowships attended by about 1,700 people every Sunday morning.

What Is an ABF?[1]

An Adult Bible Fellowship is a group or community of people committed to know and to apply the Word together in a caring fellowship. It is organized to bring about pastoral care, discipleship and outreach. It usually is divided by age groupings to enhance natural affinity and strong bonding.

In Larson's previous pastorate in Ashland, Ohio, he used an identical ABF approach to adult Sunday School. In his book, *Growing Adults on Sunday Morning*, Larson cites five purposes for the ABF.[2]

1. Fellowship—Fellowship is the number one reason people attend Sunday School, according to surveys. "They can get Bible teaching from sermons, tapes, the radio and home Bible studies," he stated. Only in ABFs do they have a broad base of fellowship.

2. Bible—Larson wants the ABF to be grounded in Bible

communication, but more than Bible content is found in most Sunday School curricula. An ABF deals with issues, practical application and answers to the problems that face adults. Those issues are approached with a biblical orientation and study.

3. Outreach—One of the primary purposes of ABF is to bring those on the fringe of the church into these smaller groups. Larson explained, "ABFs are encouraged to fish in the pool of the sanctuary." A great number of people who only casually attend church are targeted for ABF. The acceptable means is to obtain a list, to contact casual visitors and to encourage them to attend an ABF.

4. Pastoral Care—Larson is concerned about the vast number of people who are only casual visitors to The Chapel. He said that ABF employs the "Exodus 18 Principle," whereby Moses separated the people into groups of 50s and 10s for accountability and responsibility.

5. Ministry—Another purpose of ABFs is to involve more people in ministry than would be possible through the average, small Sunday School class or in the typical large church service.

What Are Adult Bible Fellowships?[3]

Some people like to call them Sunday Schools. All right. But they are more than that. They are what they say they are.

Adult: They are for college age and up, to meet their special needs.

Bible: They major on the teaching and application of the Word of God to daily living.

Fellowship: They also major on relationships and caring love, a huge need in our world.

Adult Bible Fellowships are groups for study and fellowship, organized around the Sunday morning, adult Bible study hour, often called Sunday School. They have guidelines and goals and offer much variety.

Larson believes that the Adult Bible Fellowship is the answer to a missing ingredient in most local churches: congregation.

··

A Sense of Congregation

Larson believes that the Adult Bible Fellowship is the answer to a missing ingredient in most local churches: congregation. Larson pointed out that church growth expert C. Peter Wagner calls for three groups in every New Testament church: cells, congregation and celebration.[4]

1. Celebration—Wagner says that celebration is a group of 200 or more when a church comes together to celebrate its faith and Christianity.

Larson likes to smile and say that the celebration can grow as large as 90,000 and he mentions attending a Billy Graham service where 87,000 gathered in a stadium and sang "How Great Thou Art."

The experience of a religious service in a football stadium, according to Larson, is where the Christian feels the spirit of Easter, recognizing that Christ is alive and that Christians share Resurrection joy. The celebration experience needs to be alive with enthusiasm and sincerity flowing from the heart. It is a time where people walk out with one main idea and challenge rather than being involved in a small group or having fellowship with one another.

Larson and a worship specialist plan the Sunday morning worship service at The Chapel for celebration. They want people to walk out filled with God, reverent because of the awe and majesty of God and determined in their hearts to serve Him.

2. Cell—Wagner says that a cell is the small group of 7 to 12 people who share intimacy and discipleship. The Chapel has cells to help involve people in the church.

"Cells provide a place of accountability," Larson said. In a small cell people may feel accountable to others, as well as intimate with others. In a small cell people "can ask questions...hear others and feel an atmosphere of love." An element of transparency also is present in a cell group. In a small cell people know you, your failures and strengths and love you anyway.

The Chapel has many small groups that are more than Bible studies. These are breakfast groups, discipleship groups, support groups for alcoholics, drug addicts, blended families, plus groups for single parents, college students and others with special needs.

Adult Bible Fellowships are different from the small-cell meetings. Larson used the phrase, the law of competition, which states that people won't go to two meetings designed for the same purposes twice in one week. Because of this, people won't attend a small-cell Bible study where they are learning the Word of God and come back on Sunday morning to the traditional Sunday School where they also learn the Word of God. If they are studying the Bible in the same way in both meetings, people will not attend both times. The cells miss the broader spectrum of meeting needs while the ABF misses the more narrow focus on the Word of God for study, accountability and learning.

Although hundreds of churches use the ABFs, Larson indicated that not all churches can use them unless they are willing to allow some of the pastoring to go on in these "congregations." Larson has been the speaker each year at the Moody Pastors' Conference where he teaches the concept of the ABF, helping pastors to reorganize their Sunday Schools into a more functioning purpose.

3. Congregation—Wagner says that a congregation is a

group in the church of approximately 30 to 100 people who are organized for fellowship, study, growth and outreach.

Larson stated, "I disagree with church growth people who teach that the church is made up of only the large celebration and the small cells."

Larson also disagreed with Carl George, who promotes the metachurch. George teaches that this church "revolves around two events: the meeting of small groups or cells and corporate worship or celebration."[5]

In describing his congregation as ABFs, Larson said, "We are not talking curriculum, we are not talking a way of study; an Adult Bible Fellowship is about pastoring, caring, sharing and fellowship. I want this (ABF) to be more than an old-time Sunday School class." An ABF could be called a caring system and a sharing system.

The ABF does not follow traditional curriculum. Larson said, "The beauty of Adult Bible Fellowships is that they deal with the real issues about which parents, singles and other adults feel so strongly—the need for fellowship and study."

Rather than follow the next lesson in the quarterly, the focus of Bible study comes out of the needs of the group as perceived and directed by the team of leaders, which includes the pastoral adviser, teacher, class leader and care leader.

ABF Grouping at The Chapel

The ABFs at The Chapel are grouped by affinity, which is the same as described by the Southern Baptists (i.e., age-graded and, on occasion, gender-graded). Larson noted, "I believe that people fellowship best with affinity groups—people nearly their same age and with similar interests."

The adult education pastor and the pastoral advisers direct

the teachers and leaders of ABFs by helping them choose curriculum. Curriculum is not chosen by the staff, nor is it automatically an outgrowth of a publishing house. "Our curriculum reflects the way we pastor," Larson said.

Team Selects Curriculum

The team of leaders in each ABF chooses curriculum with their pastoral adviser. The ABFs are a pastoral-focused ministry.

In this sense, they are different from the traditional church's Sunday School that falls under a Sunday School director and/or the board/committee of Christian education. The concept of ABFs began in Larson's former church. He placed the entire church into fellowships in 1971.

"We didn't vote on it," he said. "We didn't tell anybody. I began teaching a young adult class and tried to form what was, in my mind, the first Adult Bible Fellowship in the world. I remember the first year I carefully said, 'We're not going to vote on a president this year. We're going to have a class leader and I will appoint him.'"

Leaders for the Adult Bible Fellowships are selected by their spiritual gifts, commitment to Christ and their "passion."

....

Leaders Administer Class

ABF leaders are responsible to administer the class rather than the traditional class president. Next, someone is in charge of the caring system, sometimes called the care captain. The third person is the teacher, who is appointed by the pastoral staff.

At the beginning, the appointments were under the senior pastor, but that responsibility is now handled by the pastoral staff.

Most of the ABFs are conducted during the second and third worship hours. The high school Bible fellowships and singles are scheduled during the second and third hours. Because those groups prefer larger crowds, they are grouped in larger fellowships.

Leaders Selected by Spiritual Gifts

Larson says that leaders for the ABFs are selected by their spiritual gifts, commitment to Christ and their "passion" (a word that means much to him in locating spiritual gifts).

Several people are required if an ABF is to function properly. The Bible teacher communicates the lesson and helps set the mood for Bible study. He usually leads the Bible discussion.

The class leader should have a knack for organization and possess people skills. He should be comfortable in front of a crowd of 50 or more. The social chairman plans the activities and creates a social environment. Hosts, who report to the social chairman, greet the visitors and members on Sunday morning and assist with the refreshments.

Pastoral Care Is Part of Program

The care leader or couple ensures that every person in the ABF is receiving pastoral care. Those who minister under the care leaders are unit leaders who accept the pastoral responsibility and care for those in their unit.

The outreach or evangelism leader directs the outreach of the class in finding new members and giving direction to the evangelistic outreach.

All of the leaders are under a pastor, who Larson calls "the leader of the leaders." The main leaders report directly to the senior pastor or to a member of the pastoral staff. As a result, the class leaders have a pastor to whom they can turn for answers to problems or decisions.

Conclusion

The Chapel adopted the ABF program to meet the needs of its people. Because it is a large church, the ABFs provide care and personal identity to each person. Because the church is a downtown church, not a neighborhood church, the ABFs also create a feeling of oneness and ownership by each person. Because the church is growing, the ABFs are a major factor in supplying a path for growth.

Ministry Application

THE ABF STRUCTURE[6]

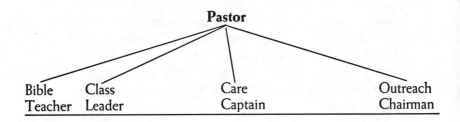

			Care Leader	Care Leader	Care Leader	
			Jones			
			Smith			
			Brown			

Pastor

Bible Teacher	Class Leader	Care Captain	Outreach Chairman
Respon-sible for Bible lessons and mood	Sunday Hours	Social Committee	Responsible for evangelistic events
	Responsible for fellowship, socials, mixing		

Responsible for pastoral care and outreach.

Reasons to Use Sunday Gatherings for the "Congregations" of the Church[7]

1. People do not have time or interest to be involved in more than two or three settings in the church.

   Where once they might have been in one worship service, another adult class, another discipleship group, another Bible study, and then a care group by neighborhood or alphabetical order or something, people simply do not have that much time or interest in that many relationships.

   Why not group them by the people with which they gather on Sunday mornings?

2. Care needs to be given in the context of friendships and Bible Study helps.

   Many churches have their care ministries revolving around a list that care leaders keep or by neighborhoods or geography. When you see people in your class, and know they are absent because you physically missed them, or you are in on the discussions on Sundays and then can relate to them in a caring way, there is more meaning to this connection. Otherwise someone is trying to show pastoral care or church love to a person they never meet with or who is simply a name.

3. There are natural settings through the ABF or adult class where you can be friends and there can be acquaintanceship as well as official care.

   Love needs time and relationships. Socials as well as Sundays and other groupings of the class help to develop this.

4. This method makes fewer lists.

   If people are on one care list and another adult Sunday School list or deacons' list, many hands can mean no work. If it is not one person's responsibility, it is probably no one's responsibility.

5. This works. Geography affinity usually does not. There are very few instances where caring by neighborhoods rather than by age affinity or gathering works.

   Arbitrary assignment usually does not work.

6. Care units within the ABF can then be developed out of natural affinities.

   Usually the care unit leaders pick the people they want to be on their list for care, and in this way they have more heart involved when they make phone calls or visit in the hospital or show other care.

NOTES

1. Knute Larson, *Growing Adults on Sunday Morning* (Wheaton, IL: Victor Books, 1991), p. 14.
2. Ibid., pp. 10,11.
3. Ibid., p. 10.
4. C. Peter Wagner, *Your Church Can Be Healthy* (Nashville, TN: Abingdon Press, 1983), p. 23.
5. Carl George, *Christianity Today*, June 24, 1991, p. 46.
6. Larson, *Growing Adults on Sunday Morning*, p. 35.
7. Ibid., p. 35.

10
Vision
Day

La Costa Hills Church
Carlsbad, California

Rev. Larry Lamb, Pastor

LARRY LAMB, A CHURCH PLANTER, MOVED TO SOUTHERN CALIFORNIA in 1989 to begin a church in the La Costa Hills area near the famous PGA West Golf Course.

Lamb targeted the baby boomers (i.e., people born between 1946 and 1964). They were upwardly mobile young families moving into the area and the husband and wife both worked. Many of those families had little or no roots in Christianity.

Lamb grew up in Amarillo, Texas, in an independent fundamentalist Baptist church that featured Southern Gospel music, evangelistic preaching and a negative stance against identified worldly sins.

But Southern California was a different world. The young couples in the area were not turned on by Country Western music and were not interested in a church that featured Southern Gospel music.

Lamb also knew they would not respond to a church that emphasized negative preaching or to one that featured evangelistic gospel preaching. He realized that a new approach would be needed to reach La Costa Hills families, and he was willing to find it.

For more than a year, while meeting young couples and holding home Bible studies, Lamb laid the foundation for a church. During this time, he attended Skyline Wesleyan Church in Lemon Grove, California, where John Maxwell was pastor.

Maxwell's contemporary ministry to the Southern California families changed Lamb's orientation. Maxwell introduced Lamb to a cross-cultural approach to ministry; he also influenced his spiritual orientation, leadership, attitudes and faith expectations.

The Focus on Vision

The La Costa Hills Church began in October 1990, in rented

facilities; a few families joined with Lamb and his wife, Heather, a Canadian he met at college.

Attendance grew slowly. On the first anniversary, 134 attended, a substantial victory in the minds of Lamb and those in the church.

In the summer of 1991, Lamb began planning a "Vision Day" that was conducted on Sunday, September 29, 1992. Lamb had attended a pastor's conference where he was encouraged to take a look at his church's future. He wanted La Costa Hills to take an honest look at the church from its past, present and future perspectives. He decided to call this time of strategizing "Vision Day."

Everyone on the Same Starting Line

"With so many people from different church backgrounds or no church background at all, I wanted everyone to know the kind of church we are," he said.

Lamb asked everyone to place a high priority on attending Vision Day. "This is more than a special church day," he said. "This is a turning point in the life of our church."

Because he felt it was so significant, the church paid for lunch, baby-sitting and valet parking at the finest resort in the area. "I want my people to expect our church to be first-class," Lamb said. "Often, Christianity is second- or third-rate." Lamb's thoughts are seconded by Jerry Falwell, who has said, "If it is Christian, it ought to be better." The resort also reflected the church's neighborhood and the kind of people who would be attracted to the church.

Power Derived from Purpose

The Sunday-morning sermon emphasized "the power of a great

purpose." Lamb pointed out that a church draws its power from its purpose. It receives great power from a great purpose.

The people ate lunch at noon, then sat around tables for the seminar format of "Vision Day."

At 1:00 P.M., Lamb pointed out that the La Costa Hills Church was concerned with relationships. "A relationship *with* Jesus Christ is a relationship of maturity *in* Jesus Christ," Lamb said in basing the discussion on Colossians 2:6,7 *(NIV)*: "So then, just as you received Christ Jesus as Lord, [that is the beginning relationship] continue to live in him, [that is in the maturing relationship] rooted and built up in him, strengthened in the faith as you were taught, and overflowing with thankfulness."

Each person had a syllabus for recording thoughts and answers. The interaction workbooks became a basis for discussions.

Vision Requires Support

Leadership is essential, Lamb pointed out, because a congregation must support the leader and the church's vision if it is to be successful.

"If we don't know what we are trying to do," Lamb said, "then we can chase ideas, programs and projects that will not produce fruit."

When everyone at the event agreed on the goal, they were shown a video by John Maxwell on *Six Keys to Church Growth.* This 58-minute video focused the attitude of the people toward a growing church. In this presentation, Maxwell emphasized six principles found in healthy churches: prayer, leadership, attitudes, evangelism, discipleship and common goals.

"What kind of church are we?" Lamb asked as he began the second session. He then presented a bar graph showing the church's year-and-a-half attendance and financial-giving records.

Future Tagged to Past

"Let's take a history lesson," Lamb explained. "We cannot properly plan for the future if we don't know our past."

This session was crucial. Lamb explained that as a church grows, the roles of the pastor and congregation change. "The pastor's hands-on ministry *decreases* and the congregation's hands-on ministry *increases*," he said.

People are willing to follow Lamb because they know what they can do, and also that he is honest with them about his weaknesses. Contemporary young adults demand credibility in leadership.

Next, Lamb explained that the pastor's and the congregation's gifts must become more clearly defined.

The "Model Church"

The "Model Church" grew out of that Vision Day session, one that would guide the ministry of the La Costa Hills Church. It is a church with:

- an inspiring vision;
- exciting goals;
- practical, proven strategies;
- a pastor who leads;
- a congregation that ministers;
- a plan that works.

Pastor Shares Weaknesses

The session ended as Lamb shared his weaknesses with the congregation. Because of the pastor's transparency, more positive comments came from the people about this session than all of the other sessions. People were willing to follow Lamb because they not only knew what he could do, but also that he was honest with them about his weaknesses. Contemporary young adults demand credibility in leadership.

In sharing his personal strengths, Lamb said, "Some leaders keep their congregation at a distance while other leaders bring the congregation in close. I love to be with people and I can motivate people to be all they can for God."

When it came to weaknesses, Lamb said, "I have a difficult time with organization and too many details cause me great confusion."

The 3:45 P.M. session was called, "Owning the Vision." This was one of the most important sessions because the people had to buy into the vision of the church if it were to succeed. They not only needed to see the vision, but also had to take ownership of the vision.

See a Vision - Buy a Vision - Own a Vision

Focus of Strategy Changes

While the purpose of La Costa Hills Church does not change, Lamb said, the focus of its strategy will. "This was crucial for present ministry and future existence," he said.

The things that will never change, Lamb said, are relationship to Jesus Christ and relationships to one another. "How will we make our vision happen?" he asked. "We need three things to happen to cause us to grow: evangelism, assimilation and care ministry."

Three Growth Ingredients
1. Evangelism/discipleship = reach out to people.
2. Assimilation = reassure people of their worth.
3. Ministry Care = respond to people in need.

Lamb said it was essential for the church to express its vision so that it was easily understood and remembered. "Let's tell people we're a REAL church," Lamb suggested.

R = Reaching the unchurched (evangelism).
E = Equipping the membership (lay ministry).
A = Assimilation of new members (assimilation).
L = Leading in church growth (leadership).

The Element of HOPE
The congregation was learning about the church, as well as learning how to set a personal vision. As a means for imprinting that vision, Lamb introduced the word HOPE. The acrostics were listed in the workbook along with places for each person to fill out the meaning. The people interacted with the acrostic and filled out the following:

H = Have a passion to reach the unchurched (evangelism).
O = Open care for hurting people (ministry).
P = Plan ways to make meaningful relationships (assimilation).
E = Express joyful celebration in worship (worship).

The pastor believed the people needed to see themselves as a church that turned inward for fellowship with one another, and also was turned outward for offering hope to others.

Then the pastor announced, "At your tables, work on these four areas by thinking of a goal and a strategy to fulfill that goal." The people began to discuss ways to carry out these four goals. As an example, they came up with questions such as:

"How can we reach more people?"

"How can we make people feel at home at La Costa Hills Church?"

"How can we take care of people?"

Without realizing it, the people were discussing the points they had heard in HOPE and in REAL.

A final recess was scheduled so people could talk to one another and build relationships.

Building a Winning Team

The final session was called, "Building a Winning Team Through a Winning Attitude."

How could the church keep its vision before the people?

First, it was decided that the church would hold membership classes in which new members would learn the vision of the church, not just discuss doctrine. In this class new members would learn their gifts, temperaments, talents and passion so they would know how to serve in this church.

The membership class was to be more than talking about church requirements. It would be a place where people were prepared to fit into ministry. A functional, new-members class was a way they could build a winning team of all new people who entered the church.

Lamb noted that people are a church's greatest assets. If they were to own the vision, there would be no room for the attitude, "It's not my responsibility to take care of people." The results: "We will all take care of one another. Every member will have a ministry."

Rethinking Past Practices

Traditional ways are available for accepting people into a church, Lamb said. People say, "Here am I. What can you do for me?" The winning attitude is, "There you are. What can I do for you?"

Returning to the theme, "Building a Winning Team," Lamb asked those people present to remember the first time they came to the church. Did they make up their minds if they would return within the first 10 minutes?

"Yes!"

Therefore, rather than permitting visitors to enter the church and to sit down, they should be invited to stand and talk to other people. Why? Because the product of the church was to be relationships.

Next, Lamb reminded them that when parents pick up their children at Sunday School, one of the first questions they ask is: "Did you have fun?" And the second question parents ask is: "What did you learn?" Parents want to make sure that their children enjoy the Sunday School and that they learn something that will influence their lives.

Church Focused on Others

Lamb pointed out that the congregation had to be a winning team with a winning attitude, and the only way to win was to be "others" focused.

"Vision Day communicates not only *what* we are going to do, but *how* we are going to do it," Lamb said. "People will not care how much we know until they know how much we care.

"We do not know the story of people who walk through the doors of our church. The most important thing is that *you are there* and with that relationship great things can happen."

"Vision Day" ended with Lamb telling a story of two boys who went to a tent revival meeting, found the tent was filled and decided to leave. An usher said, "Wait boys, I can find two seats for you in the choir area." The usher sat with them. That was the night Grady Wilson and Billy Graham accepted Christ as their Savior.

The world was changed through Billy Graham who came to Christ through a relationship, Lamb said.

Sunday School: The Foundation

The church, meanwhile, carried out its "We love children" theme through Sunday School with an action-centered curriculum based on a conservative, evangelistic curriculum.

Today, the worship service is considered the door of entry by the La Costa Hills Church, which reflects the belief and philosophy of Lamb that the primary objective is to concentrate on individual and congregational spiritual growth.

To succeed, the vision must be biblical and one that results in a biblical ministry. Where there is no vision, the church—and Sunday School—will fail.

"Vision Day" was important to the La Costa Hills Church as well as to the Sunday School. The church discovered that the greatest thing a leader can offer followers is vision. When people buy a leader's vision, they are buying into that person's leadership.

But to succeed, the vision must be biblical and one that results in a biblical ministry. Where there is no vision, the church—and Sunday School—will fail.

Ministry Application

Clearly Established Goals:
1. The goals should be worthy.
2. The goals should be attainable.
3. The goals should be measurable.

La Costa Hills Church Goals for 1993:

1. Introduce 25 people to Christ.
   The strategy: use steps a-c.

   a. Train 50 people with the "Living Proof" video series to have the confidence to build relationships with non-Christians for the purpose of evangelism. ("Living Proof" to be offered three times in 1993).
   b. Have six strategic "seeker events" that will reach the non-Christian in a natural setting. (Two men's events, two women's events, beach party, Christmas festival.)
   c. Use the information gathered from each event to continue building a positive relationship with the express purpose of presenting Christ in a natural way.

2. Have four healthy H.O.M.E. groups in operation.
   The strategy:

   a. Identify four people who desire to be a pastor of a H.O.M.E. group.
   b. Train them in leadership, pastoral care and small-group dynamics.

3. See 50 percent of the people of La Costa Hills Church involved in a specific ministry.
   The strategy:

   a. Offer three membership classes in 1993.
   b. Staff various ministries with qualified leaders who model lay ministry in action.
   c. Have bimonthly leadership meetings for all who oversee a ministry.

    d.   Emphasize lay leaders on various Sunday mornings.

4. Give $15,000 to missions.
   The strategy:

    a.   Teach on the biblical command to give.
    b.   Introduce missionaries to the congregation.

5. Have 200 first-time guests.
   The strategy:

    a.   Have 200 on our third anniversary March 21.
    b.   Have a successful Mother's Day promotion.
    c.   Invite new people.

6. Equip 15 teachers who teach with confidence to help children reach their full spiritual potential.
   The strategy:

    a.   Have training sessions twice a year.
    b.   Attend different seminars that will equip teachers.
    c.   Promote a Vacation Bible School in our community to reach 50 children.

7. Relocate to our own facility.
   The strategy:

    a.   Pray and fast.
    b.   Exercise great faith in God.
    c.   A building is only a tool. We want a building because it helps fulfill our vision.

"There is no magic in small plans. When I consider our ministry, I think of the world. Anything less than that would not be worthy of Christ nor of His will for my life."—Henrietta Mears

The Value of Mission

VISION: To take nominal Christians and to turn them into fully devoted followers of Jesus Christ.

1. It helps us be involved in a project that is larger than life.
2. It keeps us determined and devoted to God's direction.
3. It is a mental picture of what tomorrow will look like.
4. It helps develop present resources for victories tomorrow.
5. It allows us to accept losses.
6. It is a powerful expression of faith.
7. It allows us to have a focused commitment.
8. It motivates us to see people not as they are but as they can become.

11
Ninety-two Ways to Turn Around Your Sunday School

The American Sunday School movement is in trouble. It is not dying because of attacks from without but rather from inner rust and decay. In many places it has lost its direction, and as a sailing ship without wind, it is dead in the water. There are no easy answers to turn around the Sunday School; rather, the task is a tedious one.

If change is to take place, workers must perceive their tasks in a different manner and they must expect different results. Serious work is necessary to bring the Sunday School back to the place of God's full anointing. The Sunday School needs to turn around and return to its foundation. This does not refer to better education or to better ministry.

Significant changes must be made to take Sunday School back to bedrock. Those changes will be so significant that people outside the church will feel renewal and will want to attend. The changes will be so observable that those on the inside will expect greater things from the Sunday School. Ninety-two suggestions that may help accomplish that task follow.

Changes that affect perception and expectation

---

1. Change the name to Adult Bible Fellowship or Bible Study. Instead of calling it Sunday School—which suggests to outsiders that it is a place for children, a place for catechism training or a place for preparing people for church membership—call it Adult Bible Fellowship. As suggested earlier, adults are seeking fellowship based on the Bible. Obviously, those who are already in the Sunday School do not need a change of name. The title "Sunday School" is not a barrier to them; they have

accepted it and they will continue to attend. However, to the outsider, the old title could be a barrier and a new title could open the door.

2. Change the name of the Sunday School teacher to leader. Rather than giving the teacher an academic name, use a name that has more of a biblical connotation. People do not prefer another school experience that may remind them of an unpleasant past. The title "teacher" implies school. It also implies that his or her work begins when the class begins and terminates when the class ends. However, the title "leader" suggests being an example, giving care and protecting followers.

$\mathcal{J}$ob Description
Bible Study Leader
Prayer Leader
Outreach Leader
Spiritual Life Leader

On many other occasions I have used the title "shepherd" to describe a Sunday School teacher. The biblical term "shepherd" implies (1) pastoral care; (2) leadership; and (3) feeding and instructing the Word of God. Whether they are called "class leaders" or "shepherds," new titles for teachers give new expectations to class members.

3. Change the name of the secretary to receptionist. The name "secretary" implies a relationship to records and roll books. However, the primary job of the Sunday School secretary is meeting and greeting people. Therefore, the new name "receptionist" would more accurately describe receiving people and, in the process, registering them.

4. Make a new focus on Bible study with fellowship. Instead of an academic focus on what the leader does, put the focus on what the people do (i.e., study the Word of God). In studying the Bible, people ask questions, listen to their friends, talk to one another and socialize with one another. As people study the Word of God, they apply it to their lives. They listen and gain insight as questions are addressed.

5. Adapt biblical terminology. School terminology such as classrooms, chalkboards, lesson plans, lecterns, textbooks and other terms carry negative connotations. Use biblical terms such as disciplining, feeding, fellowshiping, caring, tending and learning.

6. Adopt shared leadership. Rather than the superintendent and/or a few people making all the decisions in the Sunday School, apply a new method of shared leadership. People who attend Sunday School have opinions and they want to be heard. They must feel as though they are a part of the Sunday School. Therefore, when problems need to be solved, seek the opinion of the people in the class. When decisions need to be made, seek solutions from the people in the class, and when ministry needs to be given, share it with the people in the class.

Shared Leadership
Shared Decision Making
Shared Problem Solving
Shared Ministry

---

7. Give choices of time. The Sunday School has basically demanded that everyone come at the same time and fit into the same curriculum. However, many people cannot

attend at the same time each week, and others have different preferences. Therefore, offer Sunday School at more than one time a week. The Ward Presbyterian Church in Livonia, Michigan, conducts Sunday School at 8:00 A.M., 9:00 A.M., 10:00 A.M., 11:00 A.M. and 12:30 P.M. every Sunday.

People may choose when they attend Sunday School.

The church of the future must be a cafeteria, not a plate lunch, which symbolizes that time, topic and systems of ministry have been predetermined and controlled. Just as the dietician controls what food is offered, when it is offered and how much food should be consumed, so the church of the past has controlled its curriculum, time and methods of ministry.

In the future, the church must be a cafeteria by offering choices and variety to its people, not because variety and choices are the best way to run a Sunday School, but because peoples' schedules demand more choices and variety to meet their varied needs.

Choice:
Time
Topic
Systems of Delivery

---

8. Shorten the length of lesson topics. Most Sunday Schools offer a 13-week curriculum during which one topic is discussed and developed. Traditionally, this has been called a quarter (i.e., a fourth of a year). The manual was called a quarterly. However, with the advent of television, the attention span of Americans has shortened. Because Americans are somewhat dysfunctional in this area, they

have difficulty giving attention to a topic for more than 4 to 6 weeks. Therefore, topics should be taught in series approximately one month long.

9. Recognize the distant learner/worshiper. This is the member who belongs to a church, but because of many reasons, does not attend Sunday School or church often enough to receive spiritual benefit. In the past, Sunday Schools ministered to those who were present and marked "absent" those who were not in attendance.

However, because of the time constraints, the church must be more sensitive to the distant learner/worshiper. According to surveys, the average faithful attender is in Sunday School 42 times a year. That means he/she misses 10 times a year. Two or 3 decades ago, the faithful attender/worshiper would have been there perhaps 50 times a year and would only have missed 2 or 3 times each year.

Because people are out of the area more often, Sunday School must make learning available to those who cannot be there every Sunday. People take four or five vacations each year, rather than one. They usually take multiple vacations over extended weekends. In addition, they are gone for business trips, conventions, to visit relatives or for entertainment events.

As a result, even the most faithful attender/worshiper will probably miss 10 times a year. Therefore, the Sunday School must provide videocassettes, audiocassettes and a number of other media to communicate to the distant learner/worshiper when he or she is not present.

10. Offer more practical lesson topics. The Sunday School has been driven by content because Christianity is a revelation of content about God. As a result, people were taught the content of that revelation. However, even when Sunday School has been content-bound, it has

given attention to practical application (i.e., to make the lessons work in the lives of the pupils).

Now, instead of starting with content and moving to the practical, more Sunday Schools are reversing the order. Begin where people are. Begin with practical topics and move to biblical answers. Teach how-to lessons.

11. Offer more family help. The entire church is becoming aware that we can no longer assume the strength of the family or take for granted the family's existence. We must begin offering active programs of teaching the value, purpose and strengths of the family. The three major topics that must be taught in Sunday School are: (1) husband and wife relationships; (2) parenting children; and (3) managing family finances.

12. Recognize the supernatural. We have taught the existence of the supernatural, but that knowledge has not become a part of everyday life. As American society becomes less of a Christian nation with moral laws, moral legislatures and a society that is grounded on moral values, the church will face an increasing threat from the supernatural forces of demonism and darkness. The Sunday School must equip its members to wrestle against principalities and powers, healing, deliverance from darkness and victories over pervasive habits.

Chapter 1: First Baptist Church, Arlington, Texas

13. Use Sunday School classes away from the main campus to teach the Word of God.

14. Use lay people as pastoral leaders of mission Sunday Schools.

15. Use men and women as lay leaders of Bible studies.

16. Use available space where the people are located. It may be an empty apartment, recreation room or a patio with-

out chairs. People are more important than surroundings when it comes to teaching the Word of God.

17. Use available property to teach the Word of God. Do not restrict your Bible teaching to traditional church buildings, but rather make the location serve the function of Bible teaching.

18. Make creative use of the best available time, which is Sunday morning, to teach the Word of God.

19. Do not use "barrier" titles for your Bible study.

20. Begin your ministry where your people are physically, spiritually, financially and emotionally. By meeting their needs, their hearts are open to the Word of God.

21. Recognize that clothing (i.e., "dressing up") can be a barrier for some people to attend the average American Sunday School class. Bible study leaders should be examples in appearance, yet dress to meet the needs of people.

22. Use the challenge and vision of a great opportunity to inspire workers to sacrifice.

Chapter 2: Highlands Community Church, Renton, Washington

23. Learning centers in Sunday School produce better motivation, more involvement, a larger variety of experiences and more learning in the Sunday School.

24. A team of teachers can better instruct a group of children than the isolated teacher at a table in a self-contained classroom.

25. New teachers who are recruited with purpose and focus will make a deep commitment and a continuing contribution to the Sunday School.

26. A strong commitment to children's ministry can build a total family church.

27. Men can make a strong contribution by teaching children in Sunday School.
28. Teenagers are effective as teachers in the children's department.
29. The Sunday School that believes in children will help them to grow through learning experiences based upon the Word of God.
30. Write a ministry statement (i.e., how the church will minister to its members and then employ its members in ministry).

    SAMPLE MINISTRY STATEMENT: We will present the gospel to every person in our geographical "Jerusalem," attempting to lead them to know Christ and become a member of this church. Our services are designed to help you touch God and make it possible for God to touch you. We will help you lift up the Lord through worship so He will meet your needs. We will build you up through expositional preaching of the Word of God and apply it practically so you can know His will, live every day for God, and grow to be a mature believer according to the Scriptures. We will assist you in ministering to others according to your spiritual gifts, so you can grow as a leader of others and help mature the Body of Christ.

31. Write a vision statement of what the church expects to accomplish.

    SAMPLE VISION STATEMENT: Our church is an island in a hostile world—an island where you as an individual, and your family, can come for growth in values, skills and knowledge for your various roles and duties in life. Our ministry statement reveals how we will minister to you and use you in ministry. This vision statement reveals how you will worship, study, fellowship, play, relax and celebrate the seasons of your life with other Christians so you will be strengthened, equipped and motivated to live for Christ in a hostile world. Our vision is to make you a well-rounded person as you pursue life, liberty and happiness according to God's will for your life.

Chapter 3: Saddleback Community Church, Mission Viejo, California

32. Sunday School teaching should aim at enabling people to be disciples and equipping them for ministry, rather than just Bible knowledge or doctrinal belief; it should teach skills and prepare the learner to perform a function in his or her Christian life.

33. Sunday Schools should give a sense of completion to students when they have finished a course of study, just as a high school diploma or college degree is a "statement" that the student has completed the course. Sunday School teaching tends to meander from one quarter's workbook to the next without giving the pupils a sense of completeness or arrival at a destination.

34. Pupils in Sunday School should see and work toward various levels of commitment that they will be required to attain. Most people believe that attending Sunday School is simply occupying a seat or being present to listen to a lecture. Sunday School should demand commitment from pupils at each level of attainment so they will be challenged to continued growth.

35. Sunday Schools should be willing to teach people on other days of the week and times during the day than just

on Sunday morning. Because of people's time expectations, Sunday School instruction should be made available at times other than Sunday morning.

36. The pastoral staff should understand the various levels of commitment that followers make to Christ and His Church. Then the staff should attempt to recognize where each member is located in terms of commitment and develop a strategy to move each person to a deeper commitment to Christ.

37. People will not make a deeper commitment to Christ unless leadership calls for dedication. Provide an opportunity for each person to make a deeper commitment and provide a program that will teach and allow deeper commitment.

38. A church by innovation and sacrifice can reach, teach and equip its people to become one of the largest congregations in America without permanent worship and education facilities.

39. A pastor's primary focus is recruiting, training, leading and motivating the pastoral staff to ministry.

Chapter 4: Florence Baptist Temple, Florence, South Carolina

40. Sunday Schools should reemphasize enrollment because it tells the pupils that they "belong" to the class and to other people, hence bonding them to the local church.

41. The Sunday School should be organized through enrollment so that people feel an obligation to the class, to other believers in the class and to reach out to those who should and could be in the class. Sunday Schools that just expect people to attend are probably weak in follow-up of absentees, weak in outreach to others who need to

be in the class and weak in demanding commitment to Christ and His Church.

42. Sunday Schools should return to an emphasis of enrollment because it gives a natural "stairstepping" process to bring people into the influence of the church where the Word of God can perform the work of God in their lives. Those who have been enrolled in Sunday School are in a place where they can be "stairstepped" to Christ.

43. Sunday Schools that actively seek to enroll people in Bible study are actually securing the permission of the nonchurched person to minister to them, bringing them into a place of conversion, growth in Christ and usefulness in the church.

44. Sunday Schools should organize an approach to enrollment so that barriers that keep people from Bible study are removed and doors are opened for people to participate in class fellowship and to study the Word of God.

45. Small adult classes make it easier for members to discuss the lesson, to answer questions and to apply the lesson to daily life.

46. The formation of additional adult classes will make it easier for more adults to find a place of group leadership, hence equipping them for service.

Chapter 5: Second Baptist Church, Houston, Texas

47. Sunday School classes should be encouraged to grow larger in attendance because many adults want to attend a class that has a number of activities and functions.

48. Sunday Schools should seek teachers who have the strongest gift of communicating the Word of God.

49. Those people with the spiritual gift of leadership should lead the class. This is not necessarily the same role as the class teacher nor the class shepherd. The class leader

should have managing skills so that he can get many members involved in the class, making the class a functioning group of every member ministering to one another.

50. Organize Sunday School classes with a view of involving every person in Christian service. People do not automatically volunteer for service nor find a place of service; rather people must be identified, sought, trained and involved in Christian service.

51. Allow men and women to minister in the Sunday School according to the New Testament principles for ministry. Because the Sunday School teacher is the extension of the pastoral ministry, the pastor and staff reflect the direction and responsibility of the New Testament content that is taught. Therefore, men and women can be shepherds/leaders of adult Sunday School classes to carry out the purpose of the pastoral staff and the church.

52. Recognize that modern young adults want team leadership in areas of management. They want to be part of a team in their Sunday School classes for shared goal setting, shared decision making and shared problem solving. This gives the Sunday School the strength of many differently gifted people, yet the direction of the Word of God.

53. Sunday School teachers and leaders should be appointed by the senior pastor and/or the pastoral staff because the Sunday School teacher is the extension of the pastoral ministry into the life of the class.

Chapter 6: First Assembly of God, Phoenix, Arizona

54. Sunday School busing still works when people will work at it.

55. The success of Sunday School busing depends on the vision of the leader who has great passion to make it work.

56. The success of Sunday School busing begins with com-

mitment and passion, not techniques or the method of how it is done.

57. The vision of reaching a great number of people will cause workers to sacrifice and to make a commitment to reach that goal.

58. Facilities (buildings) and tools (buses) are only means to the vision; they are not mandatory for the vision.

59. A Sunday School can have fantastic growth of unrealistic proportions when it is driven by a gigantic vision.

60. The continuing force that drives a Sunday School bus ministry is soul-winning and evangelism. The reward of people won to Christ is a dynamic that keeps a Sunday School bus ministry alive.

61. Spiritual power for conversion and supply of money grows out of vision; it does not come before vision.

62. The synergistic principle of many forces producing multiple growth still takes place in a church when busing is combined with a variety of other dynamic principles to attract people, to present the gospel to them and to call for a commitment to Jesus Christ.

63. A compassion to alleviate the misery of people (HIV victims, rape victims, homeless, etc.) is still a strong dynamic to attract people to the teaching of the Word of God.

Chapter 7: Grove City Church of the Nazarene, Grove City, Ohio

64. A Sunday evening Sunday School is an excellent alternative when the traditional evening service is not well attended and the members do not respond to a second sermon or second worship service on Sunday evening.

65. A Sunday evening Sunday School provides "unpressured" time for Bible study and fellowship because members

don't have to rush from Bible study to a worship service.

66. A Sunday evening Sunday School allows the pastoral staff to focus more time and attention (not to mention adding additional space for worship services) on Sunday morning without trying to sandwich in a morning Sunday School.

67. A Sunday evening Sunday School allows the worshiper, especially the family with young children, time to attend church on Sunday morning without pressure to get up and get dressed. The member is able to prepare and to focus his or her heart for worship before arriving at the church.

68. A Sunday evening Sunday School relieves pressure from the dedicated Christian who serves in Sunday School and/or worship so they can better focus on the separate purpose of the morning and evening activities.

Chapter 8: Skyline Wesleyan Church, Lemon Grove, California

69. The commitment to evangelism and outreach will cause a church to grow, not the provision of extra classroom space by adding additional services.

70. Because traditional Christians are usually resistant to change, the leader must give the "big picture" of the church's vision and mission if the congregation is to accept the addition of extra Sunday School sessions.

71. The entire church must recognize the benefits of an additional Sunday School before it will work.

72. In an age of prohibitive building costs, a church should not automatically rule out an additional Sunday School but should carefully study the advantages and practical techniques that an additional Sunday School will offer.

73. When beginning an additional Sunday School, the staff should think long range and should prepare the people

for the stress that occurs during the "change valley."

74. The staff that supervises Sunday School should be careful of "double dipping," (i.e., using volunteer workers twice because they are easier to enlist than it would be to recruit and train new workers for the additional Sunday School).

75. Those leaders who initiate an additional Sunday School should be prepared for criticism because it will be tougher to establish than most people expect and it will take longer to initiate than expected.

76. The key to successfully beginning an additional Sunday School is support from the pulpit.

Chapter 9: The Chapel, Akron, Ohio

77. The adult Sunday School will not be revitalized by emphases on curriculum and new, inspired ways of teaching, but rather by emphasizing relationships among class members and by focusing Bible study on the needs of class members.

78. Because the teacher is the extension of pastoral care to the adult class, the pastor should appoint those leaders who will carry out pastoral care and will organize the adult Bible fellowship to extend his ministry.

79. The modern Adult Bible Fellowship is led by a team of leaders, each of whom will focus on one function such as leading Bible study, leading outreach, leading in pastoral care, leading in fellowship and leading the class.

80. The Adult Bible Fellowship fulfills the congregational needs of the church where cells fulfill the intimacy needs and church worship fulfills the need for celebration.

81. Adult Bible Fellowships make it possible for the pastor to delegate his "watchcare" ministry to members and places where that responsibility is carried out adequately.

82. Because people will not return to receive the same ministry a second time each week, the cell is designed for

deep Bible study and the congregation (Adult Bible Fellowship) is designed for discussion of relevant topics from a biblical perspective.

83. Because believers are nurtured by a caring person and by warm, receptive groups, the Adult Bible Fellowship can be a nurturing community for all.

84. Because people fellowship best with affinity groups (people nearly the same age and similar interests), the Adult Bible Fellowships should be organized around these catalysts.

Chapter 10: La Costa Hills Church, Carlsbad, California

85. Plan a "Vision Day." This will start all workers at the same place and headed in the same direction. Vision gives strength to workers and to the church.

86. Vision helps a new church get all people and workers on the same footing.

87. Vision encourages people to cooperate and produces commitment to the church.

88. Vision is more important for a new work than is the method used to establish the new church.

89. Vision involves what a church is, where it is going, how it will get there and what methods it will use to reach that destination.

90. A vision statement (where the church is going) is just as important as a ministry statement (how it will do ministry) and a doctrinal statement (what it believes).

91. The person who supplies the vision to a church is the actual leader of the church.

92. When people do not accept the vision of the leader, they have rejected his leadership. Even if he is called a leader and functions as a leader, he is not the leader.

12
Resources

THE ITEMS LISTED WITH EACH CHURCH ARE SUGGESTIONS FOR further study on the topic. They are also programs that will help in successfully implementing the ideas.

Chapter 1

Lewis, Larry. *The Church Planter's Handbook*. Broadman Press, Nashville, TN, 1992. This book, written by the president of the Home Mission Board, Southern Baptist Convention, is directed at church planting but touches on mission planting that is done by the First Baptist Church, Arlington, Texas.

Chapter 2

Gospel Light Sunday School Curriculum, 2300 Knoll Drive, Ventura, CA 93003, 1-800-4-GOSPEL. This company is dedicated and oriented to excellence in children's curriculum.

Towns, Elmer. *Towns' Sunday School Encyclopedia*. Tyndale House Publishers, Wheaton, IL, 1993. See article on children's class, how to teach children.

Chapter 3

Church Growth Institute, P.O. Box 4404, Lynchburg, VA 24502. Church Growth Institute offers four curriculum resource packets designed for a church's new members' class in finances, lay involvement, doctrine and lay leadership. Each packet contains audio lessons, textbook, worksheets, etc.

Gospel Light Publications, 2300 Knoll Drive, Ventura, CA 93003. This Sunday School curriculum is age-guided, Bible-based and Christ-centered. It is relevant to modern problems and uses up-to-date art and printing displays. Because of its excellence, every church should examine this literature. For samples, phone 1-800-4-GOSPEL.

Towns, Elmer. *Towns' Sunday School Encyclopedia*. Tyndale House Publishers, Wheaton, IL, 1993. See articles on curriculum, teaching materials, etc.

Warren, Rick, 23456 Madero, Suite 100, Mission Viejo, CA 92691, 1-714-581-5683. The curriculum used at Saddleback Valley Community Church and tapes describing the church's strategy may be ordered.

Chapter 4

Towns, Elmer. *Sunday School Enrollment.* Church Growth Institute, P.O. Box 4404, Lynchburg, VA 24502. This is a resource packet to teach adult Sunday School classes the value, strategy and practical steps to implement an enrollment program in a church. This resource packet contains audiocassette, textbook, worksheets, publicity, etc. An optional video for classroom teaching is available. This packet takes strategy used by Southern Baptists and applies it for non-Southern Baptist churches.

Towns, Elmer. *Towns' Sunday School Encyclopedia.* Tyndale House Publishers, Wheaton, IL, 1993. See the article on Sunday School enrollment.

Chapter 5

Towns, Elmer. *Ten of Today's Most Innovative Churches.* Regal Books, Ventura, CA, 1990. See chapter on the Second Baptist Church.

Towns, Elmer. *Towns' Sunday School Encyclopedia.* Tyndale House Publishers, Wheaton, IL, 1993. See the chapter on young adult, singles and adult classes.

Chapter 6

Barnett, Tommy. *The Successful Bus Director's Book.* Phoenix First Assembly, 13613 North Cave Creek, Phoenix, AZ

85022-5137, 1-602-867-7117. This book provides step-by-step guidelines on the responsibilities of being a bus director.

Beebe Publications, P.O. Box 659, Stockbridge, GA 30281, 1-800-828-4595. This organization offers books on the principles and practical methods of making a bus ministry work. It also has a full range of resources to support a bus ministry.

Chapter 7

Towns, Elmer. *How to Go to Two Services.* Church Growth Institute, P.O. Box 4404, Lynchburg, VA 24502. This resource packet has a video that can be shown to the board and other organizations in the church with a view of getting their approval and support to add an additional worship service or Sunday School hour. Although not aimed at beginning an evening Sunday School, this resource will help the pastor plan additional services or to alter existing services.

Chapter 8

Maxwell, John. *Be All You Can Be*, 1530 Jamacha Road, Suite D, El Cajon, CA 92019-3757. Through the Injoy Club, John Maxwell offers a monthly leadership cassette tape in which he teaches his church staff leadership principles. It contains a worksheet for the listener to evaluate and to improve a person's leadership skills.

Maxwell, John. *Winning Attitude.* Injoy Publishing Co., El Cajon, CA. This resource is available through the Injoy Club.

Towns, Elmer. *Ten of Today's Most Innovative Churches.* Regal Books, Ventura, CA, 1990. Chapter 1 features the principles John Maxwell follows in making innovative changes in his church. This is an excellent role model to examine when studying how to make changes at a church.

Chapter 9

Dean, Rodney, and McIntosh, Gary. *How to Start or Evaluate a Small Group Ministry.* Church Growth Institute, P.O. Box 4404, Lynchburg, VA 24502. This interactive manual is designed to help the pastor of any size church set up a small-group ministry or to evaluate an existing ministry.

Larson, Knute. *Growing Adults on Sunday Morning.* Victor Books, Wheaton, IL, 1991. The pastor of The Chapel on University Hill describes the Adult Bible Fellowships that are used in this church.

Wagner, C. Peter. *Your Church Can Be Healthy.* Abingdon Press, Nashville, TN, 1983.

Chapter 10

Barna, George. *The Power of Vision.* Regal Books, Ventura, CA, 1992. This is the best book written on the power that leaders derive from vision.

Maxwell, John. *Six Keys to Church Growth.* Charles E. Fuller Evangelistic Association, P.O. Box 91990, Pasadena, CA, 1990. In this resource packet, Maxwell teaches the essentials of prayer, leadership, evangelism, discipleship, lay ministry and goals in building a church.

Towns, Elmer. *Ten of Today's Most Innovative Churches.* Regal Books, Ventura, CA, 1990. This is a study of leadership in 10 churches.

Towns, Elmer. *America's Fastest Growing Churches.* Impact Books, Nashville, TN, 1972. A study of 10 churches that grew rapidly in the early '70s, each primarily using a bus ministry. However, chapter 12 is a study of charismatic leadership (not related to signs and wonders but to the power of personality in leadership). This chapter examines more than 20 doctrinal dissertations in determining the makeup of powerful, effective leadership.

Towns, Elmer. *The Eight Laws of Leadership.* Church Growth Institute, P.O. Box 4404, Lynchburg, VA 24502, 1993. This is a textbook on leadership for the resource packet, *Team Leadership.* This resource packet for pastors offers instruction on leadership to lay people. It contains video lessons, textbook, worksheets, etc.

13
Comparison
of Statistics

𝒥HE STATISTICS IN THE FOLLOWING 12 CHARTS WERE SUPPLIED BY the 10 Sunday Schools reviewed in this book and were compiled for study and analysis.

They are presented for the serious student who wishes to conduct research in these churches to discover some of the causes and results of innovative trends and programs.

CHURCH MEMBERSHIP

CHURCH	1980	1985	1990	1992
First Baptist Church Arlington, TX	5,746	6,401	7,092	7,528
Highlands Community Church Renton, WA	313	476	568	599
Saddleback Valley Community Church Mission Viejo, CA	N/A	615	1,808	3,245
Florence Baptist Temple Florence, SC	2,111	2,689	3,157	3,367
Second Baptist Church Houston, TX	5,128	9,138	16,649	19,274
First Assembly of God Phoenix, AZ	N/A	N/A	N/A	N/A
Grove City Church of the Nazarene Grove City, OH	439	554	721	857
Skyline Wesleyan Church Lemon Grove, CA	1,462	1,829	2,485	N/A
The Chapel Akron, OH	6,000	6,400	6,700	7,000
La Costa Hills Church Carlsbad, CA	0	0	54	85

AVERAGE WORSHIP ATTENDANCE

CHURCH	1980	1985	1990	1992
First Baptist Church Arlington, TX	1,168	1,150	1,267	1,368
Highlands Community Church, Renton, WA	543	595	669	774
Saddleback Valley Community Church Mission Viejo, CA	146	219	3,823	5,025
Florence Baptist Temple Florence, SC	850	902	1,060	1,280
Second Baptist Church Houston, TX	1,583	4,425	8,476	9,444
First Assembly of God Phoenix, AZ	N/A	N/A	N/A	N/A
Grove City Church of the Nazarene Grove City, OH	370	440	674	897
Skyline Wesleyan Church, Lemon Grove, CA	1,133	2,044	3,128	N/A
The Chapel Akron, OH	N/A	3,300	3,802	4,501
La Costa Hills Church Carlsbad, CA	0	0	40	64

AVERAGE SUNDAY SCHOOL ATTENDANCE

CHURCH	1980	1985	1990	1992
First Baptist Church Arlington, TX	1,550	1,820	2,819	3,919
Highlands Community Church, Renton, WA	517	611	735	801
Saddleback Valley Community Church Mission Viejo, CA	N/A	585	4,260	4,919
Florence Baptist Temple Florence, SC	1,406	1,315	1,126	1,180
Second Baptist Church Houston, TX	1,066	2,882	5,583	9,412
First Assembly of God Phoenix, AZ	N/A	N/A	N/A	N/A
Grove City Church of the Nazarene Grove City, OH	360	376	514	569
Skyline Wesleyan Church Lemon Grove, CA	1,355	1,618	2,597	N/A
The Chapel Akron, OH	N/A	N/A	2,988	3,234
La Costa Hills Church Carlsbad, CA	0	0	18	27

AVERAGE CHILDREN'S SUNDAY SCHOOL ATTENDANCE

CHURCH	1980	1985	1990	1992
First Baptist Church Arlington, TX	242	209	208	234
Highlands Community Church Renton, WA	212	259	428	493
Saddleback Valley Community Church Mission Viejo, CA	N/A	250	1,901	2,866
Florence Baptist Temple Florence, SC	N/A	N/A	276	300
Second Baptist Church Houston, TX	224	537	1,020	1,817
First Assembly of God Phoenix, AZ	N/A	N/A	N/A	N/A
Grove City Church of the Nazarene, Grove City, OH	95	87	171	236
Skyline Wesleyan Church Lemon Grove, CA	498	540	861	N/A
The Chapel Akron, OH	N/A	N/A	1,250	1,390
La Costa Hills Church Carlsbad, CA	0	0	18	27

AVERAGE YOUTH SUNDAY SCHOOL ATTENDANCE

CHURCH	1980	1985	1990	1992
First Baptist Church Arlington, TX	180	209	167	156
Highlands Community Church Renton, WA	68	79	91	100
Saddleback Valley Community Church Mission Viejo, CA	N/A	90	201	350
Florence Baptist Temple Florence, SC	N/A	N/A	259	280
Second Baptist Church Houston, TX	837	2,076	3,658	7,225
First Assembly of God Phoenix, AZ	N/A	N/A	N/A	N/A
Grove City Church of the Nazarene Grove City, OH	60	65	56	91
Skyline Wesleyan Church Lemon Grove, CA	267	214	261	N/A
The Chapel Akron, OH	N/A	N/A	462	419
La Costa Hills Church Carlsbad, CA	0	0	0	5

Average Adult Sunday School Attendance

CHURCH	1980	1985	1990	1992
First Baptist Church Arlington, TX	820	876	1,001	1,009
Highlands Community Church Renton, WA	237	237	216	208
Saddleback Valley Community Church Mission Viejo, CA	N/A	245	2,152	1,703
Florence Baptist Temple Florence, SC	375	400	443	450
Second Baptist Church Houston, TX	100	272	449	738
First Assembly of God Phoenix, AZ	N/A	N/A	N/A	N/A
Grove City Church of the Nazarene Grove City, OH	205	224	287	242
Skyline Wesleyan Church Lemon Grove, CA	587	862	1,396	N/A
The Chapel Akron, OH	400	500	1,276	1,425
La Costa Hills Church Carlsbad, CA	0	0	0	0

TOTAL INCOME

CHURCH	1980	1985	1990	1992
First Baptist Church Arlington, TX	$1,546,293	$2,638,551	$3,728,308	$4,310,530
Highlands Community Church Renton, WA	753,501	811,793	1,285,322	1,285,945
Saddleback Valley Community Church Mission Viejo, CA	N/A	47,000	555,000	2,932,000
Florence Baptist Temple, Florence, SC	654,721	961,847	1,219,574	1,429,214
Second Baptist Church Houston, TX	N/A	14,000,000	17,500,000	21,600,000
First Assembly of God Phoenix, AZ	N/A	N/A	N/A	N/A
Grove City Church of the Nazarene Grove City, OH	206,817	377,778	776,566	1,002,068
Skyline Wesleyan Church Lemon Grove, CA	762,315	1,644,177	3,871,456	4,026,344
The Chapel Akron, OH	N/A	N/A	N/A	N/A
La Costa Hills Church Carlsbad, CA	0	0	39,940	87,791

NUMBER OF CONVERSIONS

CHURCH	1980	1985	1990	1992
First Baptist Church Arlington, TX	128	89	180	136
Highlands Community Church Renton, WA	N/A	N/A	376	118
Saddleback Valley **Community Church** Mission Viejo, CA	N/A	N/A	N/A	N/A
Florence Baptist Temple Florence, SC	341	172	120	114
Second Baptist Church Houston, TX	N/A	501	1,024	974
First Assembly of God Phoenix, AZ	N/A	N/A	N/A	N/A
Grove City Church **of the Nazarene** Grove City, OH	114	190	210	222
Skyline Wesleyan Church Lemon Grove, CA	519	358	760	N/A
The Chapel Akron, OH	N/A	N/A	N/A	N/A
La Costa Hills Church Carlsbad, CA	0	0	2	10

NUMBER OF BAPTISMS

CHURCH	1980	1985	1990	1992
First Baptist Church Arlington, TX	128	89	180	136
Highlands Community Church Renton, WA	38	39	36	30
Saddleback Valley Community Church Mission Viejo, CA	N/A	127	295	508
Florence Baptist Temple Florence, SC	161	91	115	84
Second Baptist Church Houston, TX	N/A	439	1,008	887
First Assembly of God Phoenix, AZ	N/A	N/A	N/A	N/A
Grove City Church of the Nazarene Grove City, OH	10	12	13	21
Skyline Wesleyan Church Lemon Grove, CA	183	105	112	119
The Chapel Akron, OH	N/A	N/A	N/A	N/A
La Costa Hills Church Carlsbad, CA	0	0	0	12

CHURCH	TV Ministry No. of Stations	Radio Ministry No. of Stations	Outreach Program Plan Followed	No. of Visits Per Week No. Involved	K-12 Day School No. Enrolled
First Baptist Church Arlington, TX	2	0	Weekly	75 60	9 K. only
Highlands Community Church, Renton, WA	0	0	use their own	6-15 10	N/A
Saddleback Valley Community Church Mission Viejo, CA	0	0		35 49	N/A
Florence Baptist Temple Florence, SC	1 station 2 cable stations		Reach, Teach, Win, Disciple	300 200	572
Second Baptist Church Houston, TX	28 stations	0	use their own	323 463	1,037
First Assembly of God Phoenix, AZ					
Grove City Church of the Nazarene Grove City, OH	0	0	"loaf of love," evangelism phone, etc.	20-25 visits per week	120
Skyline Wesleyan Church Lemon Grove, CA	0	0	use their own	9 50	N/A
The Chapel Akron, OH	1 local	1 local	follow up visitors	1-200 40-50	N/A
La Costa Hills Church Carlsbad, CA	0	0			

CHURCH	Building Value	Seating Capacity	Acreage Attached to Church	Parking Spaces	Denomination	Cell Group(s) Attendance
First Baptist Church Arlington, TX	8,700,000	2,000	8.5	2,730 3 block radius	Southern Baptist	N/A
Highlands Community Church Renton, WA	$2,068,000	550	7.5	300	Non-denom-inational	350 total
Saddleback Valley Community Church Mission Viejo, CA	$185,000 (tent)	2,200 (tent)	76	1,500	Southern Baptist	1,270
Florence Baptist Temple, Florence, SC	$7,500,000	1,700	39	625	Inde-pendent Baptist	12-15 in each class
Second Baptist Church, Houston, TX	$85,000,000	6,200	32	2,500	Southern Baptist	0
First Assembly of God Phoenix, AZ	N/A	N/A	N/A	N/A	N/A	N/A
Grove City Church of the Nazarene Grove City, OH	$4,000,000	1,000	54	300	Church of the Nazarene	200 total (24 groups)
Skyline Wesleyan Church Lemon Grove, CA	$6,413,809	1,000	9	900	Wesleyan	1,400
The Chapel Akron, OH		2,100	38	1,000	Inde-pendent	80-120 groups
La Costa Hills Church Carlsbad, CA	using rental facilities	150	none	160	North American Baptist	32 total (2 groups)

CHURCH	No. of Children's S.S. Teachers/ Workers	No. of Youth S.S Teachers/ Workers	No. of Adult S.S. Teachers/ Workers
First Baptist Church Arlington, TX	65	39	185
Highlands Community Church Renton, WA	145	30	10
Saddleback Valley Community Church Mission Viejo, CA	360	33	81
Florence Baptist Temple Florence, SC	112	40	185
Second Baptist Church Houston, TX	1,174	57	1,701
First Assembly of God Phoenix, AZ	N/A	N/A	N/A
Grove City Church of the Nazarene Grove City, OH	30	14	13
Skyline Wesleyan Church Lemon Grove, CA	176	36	47
The Chapel Akron, OH	891	35	35 ABFs
La Costa Hills Church Carlsbad, CA	10	1	no adult Sunday School